Reviews

"*Awake Beloved and Arise: Transforming Suffering Into Strength* is written with inspiration, authority and honesty by one who understands because she has traveled the road. In this book Linda Huntzinger Calhoun draws deeply, wisely from the best and brightest minds. Out of that abundance she has fashioned a message of her own, one that will provide counsel and consolation for all those fortunate enough to read it."

> – Dean Duncan, PhD Glasgow University; Associate Professor, Theater Arts & Media, Brigham Young University

"This is an engaging, honest book, with stories and principles that inspired me to think more deeply about how adversity has helped me to nurture my strengths and become who I am today. It helped me to be more accepting of imperfection in myself, and left me feeling empowered to make changes. Since struggle is universal, this book will be helpful to a wide audience!"

> – Amber P., Group Leader for FindingHope.org (The Younique Foundation, providing hope and support for survivors of childhood sexual abuse)

"This book is nothing short of inspirational. It has the insights, stories, examples and tools to help anyone trying to make changes in their behavior so they can move forward into a more satisfying future. The author has done a beautiful job of showing how, if you are willing, you can heal from past wounds and create a better life."

> – Kathleen Parish, Mother and Survivor of Life

Awake
Beloved
AND
Arise

Awake
Beloved
AND

Arise

TRANSFORMING
SUFFERING INTO
STRENGTH

Linda Huntzinger Calhoun

Permissions:

From *Life of Pi* by Yann Martel (Harcourt, 2001) © 2001 Yann Martel. With permission of the author.

MERE CHRISTIANITY by C. S. Lewis copyright © C. S. Lewis Pte. Ltd. 1942, 1943, 1944, 1952. Extract printed by permission.

The Younique Foundation, for concepts from *Reclaim Hope: Empowering Your Life Through Five Strategies* © 2016. Used with permission.

ISBN: 978-1-09830-133-0
eBook ISBN: 978-1-09830-134-7

Printed in the United States of America

Mountain Muse Studio
Provo, Utah

Dedicated To

Shelley, Natalie, Aaron, Rebecca, Jared,
Kathryn (Kate), Daniel and Mark:

for the joy and blessing you are,

for your strength and perception,

for the good you are contributing to the world

and for the opportunity to be your mother
and share the journey with you

Contents

Acknowledgements

The first acknowledgement goes to Susan Keippel. Susan's invitation to meet, the conversations of that marvelous week and the memory of her teen-age imagination seeing the Sleeping Maiden arise from her mountaintop were the catalyst that sparked this book into being. Exactly what it was to be remained vague, until suddenly one day the focus and framework came clearly to my mind, complete with a detailed outline. Another book emerged from Susan's specific expertise.

To my talented writing critique group, Refiner's Fire: Betty Briggs, Sherri Curtis, Phyllis Gunderson, Norma Mitchell, Bradley Estel and Rene' Murdock, Linda Orvis and Karen Pool, a tremendous thank you. Your support has been essential.

A special thank you to my children, who are loved beyond words and from whom I continue to learn. May the concepts and stories here aid you, your dear families and those who come after.

Kathy, my cousin and dear friend, our conversations sorting things out are irreplaceable, and *so* important. A special nod to Soren Olsen and his parents, Poul Erik and Kirsten: you didn't know what was going on in my life, but your esteem and caring kept me afloat during a critical, dark time. Thanks to Doug and Diana Holt, who gently helped me first begin to deal with some hard realities. To my Beta Readers: your discernment, encouragement and enthusiasm have been wonderfully helpful and much appreciated. An especial thank you to Linda and Ted Sandstrom—they know why. And to Karen and Stan Pool, to Ron Rencher and Randy Calhoun, who have been an ongoing, sustaining support, love always.

Also, love and appreciation to many other friends who have been supportive during the creative process and eager to see the finished work. To all of you, your interest and encouragement matters more than you know. Thank you all, dear friends.

Most important, gratitude to God, who fills my life with blessings. He initiated this undertaking, gave me courage, and has directed and supported me throughout. His grace is as necessary as breathing.

Introduction

After seven years from conception to completion, this manuscript arrived at the publishers in early 2020. Then the world turned upside down. A deadly, highly contagious new virus emerged in China and quickly engulfed the whole planet. Usually bustling, crowded city streets in every country were eerily empty and silent as people isolated at home for safety. Hospitals and morgues were strained beyond capacity, with millions dying from COVID-19. Outraged demonstrations in response to vicious racial discrimination in the U.S. ignited angry protests world-wide. Record-setting wildfires destroyed forests, homes, lives and more than 4.4 million acres of forestland in California alone. Climate change and melting polar ice caps continued to accelerate at an alarming rate. Political turmoil in the U.S. brought sharply divisive viewpoints into high relief, with concerns of violence which materialized. 2020 was a year of fear, anger, sorrow and turbulence. Now well into 2021, much of it continues.

Yet there is hope. Effective vaccines against Covid-19 were quickly developed and started being administered by the end of 2020. Resourceful people are finding and will find new, creative ways to solve problems and help one another, as they have always done. The world's troubles are real and serious, but there is great strength, goodness and courage in humanity. As there is in you.

Wherever you are in your life, this book is written to enable you to awaken and arise to become the powerful Shining Warrior you are meant to be. Difficult challenges come to everyone, and many feel especially disadvantaged by background, race, gender, life experiences, and financial and educational situations. These are impactful influences. Yet they need not permanently define or confine us. In these pages you will find stories, concepts, and tools to help you in your unique personal quest to create the life you desire.

The genesis of this book came about when Susan and I met in a mountain valley for the first time in ten years, the shining sheet of Utah Lake gleaming silver to the west, the rugged bulwarks of the Wasatch Mountains soaring to the north and east—a stunning setting for a happy reunion. We had become friends more than 20 years earlier in Tucson, Arizona when our children were growing up together. A few years later I moved away. For this meeting Susan traveled up from Tucson and I came from Northern California. Talking almost non-stop, we shared joys and sorrows, challenges and victories, and what it all meant.

Life has not been easy. We realized that from our own personal experience or in the lives of people we love, we have dealt with the challenges of family systems which supported emotional, physical and sexual abuse; marriage and parenting;

divorce; disabling chronic illness; single motherhood; gender identity issues; poverty; mental illness; addiction; crisis of faith; death of loved ones, and more.

Even though our lives vary widely in the details and while learning continues, we found we had both arrived at a similar place of understanding and peace. We had learned deeply important truths from our experiences and recognized their value not only to ourselves, but their potential to help others. At one electrifying point it was made absolutely clear that these insights were to result in a book.

Two books evolved: this authored by me, and *ABC's for Families*, addressing the details of early childhood environment and development, by Susan Keippel. While Susan's Master's Degree encompassed human development throughout the span of life, it focused specifically on early childhood. She has extensive professional experience in working with families with young children.

My B.A. is in the Humanities with an Emphasis in Writing. My professional experience includes Interior Design, which was my original field of study and pure fun. Over time I shifted focus, and as an Adjunct Professor taught classes for students and presented workshops in Personal and Professional Development to corporate, college, city and state leadership groups. I am an instructor at our County Jail, and you will hear some of the inmate's stories—hopefully you will never experience incarceration, but there are things to learn from those in that situation. This book shares experiences of individuals from many different walks of life, and a few of my own.

Suffering is something everyone understands. How do we turn its pain into life-enhancing strength and happiness? It can be done. If current or past distress is hindering your present, it is time to awaken and create a new future. The stories and examples shared here are true. To protect privacy different names will most often be used. You may recognize your own situation in some of the stories, if so, use them as a catalyst for your own healing.

This is a faith-based book, and as author I take responsibility for its content. Among my friends are people who are Hindu, Jewish, Muslim, agnostic, atheist, and a variety of Christian denominations. I am a Christian, joyfully a member of The Church of Jesus Christ of Latter-day Saints. I count as friends those from a wide spectrum of race, ethnicity and country of origin as well as a variety of genders. Such differences are irrelevant to good character and integrity, which are found among all people everywhere. Whatever your personal belief system may be, you have the right to believe as you choose and to be treated with respect. That will be honored here. As a reader, the same will be expected of you.

In the healing disciplines evidence is strong that for many people, belief in some kind of a higher power greater than oneself is a potent source of strength and comfort. It has been true for me. As have countless others, I have felt the sustaining, guiding hand of a loving God, teaching me to value myself, my experience, and my place as an individual of great worth. This knowledge is empowering, healing, and truly priceless. Whether you realize it yet or not, you are also an individual of tremendous worth, with valuable contributions to make. No one can replace you or duplicate what you have to offer. I pray that this book will give you knowledge, confidence and tools to assist you in your unique and profoundly important journey.

Flashes of understanding can slip away quickly, so you may want to read with a pen or highlighter in hand. There are blank pages at the back if you need more room for notes.

The information here is applicable and equally important to both men and women. Gentlemen, you and your fine masculine qualities are greatly appreciated and admired. This book however, comes from a female perspective, since that comes most naturally to me.

All of us experience wounds. A wealth of information supporting the healing process exists, and the appendix offers a treasure trove of additional reading. Each writer offers their own perspective, each perhaps speaks to a different need— what resonates with you will depend upon where you are on your own unique path. You will recognize what is most valuable to you at the time you need it. Trust yourself, and trust the journey—it supports a glorious future!

One

The Story Of The Sleeping Maiden

"For each of us, there comes a time when we must awaken and become what we were born to become."

.... Seth Adam Smith, <u>Rip Van Winkle and the Pumpkin Lantern</u>

As we visited, Susan and I found ourselves often gazing at Mount Timpanogos, a massive monolith rising nearly 12,000 feet above sea level. Its craggy crest forms the profile of The Sleeping Maiden. She is reclining on her back, her hands folded across her chest, her long hair flowing out behind. She has been there for eons.

Looking at this dramatic vista, Susan mused, "I saw the Sleeping Maiden for the first time when I was a young teen visiting from Arizona. I envisioned her sitting up, then standing and looking around, and . . . walking off."

"Oh!" I exclaimed, "That is exactly what we're talking about—waking up, standing tall, and moving into a better future!"

Idea built upon excited idea, all affirming this truth: every human being, male and female, has hidden within them a magnificent Shining Warrior waiting to awaken. It is the vital, dynamic core in each of us. Until it does we slumber, unaware and unknowing. When we wake up and become aware, we can identify what we want and move forward with strength and purpose into accomplishment. The Sleeping Maiden became the symbol of that process.

So imagine now the living Sleeping Maiden, waking up amidst the clouds wreathing her mountaintop. She stirs, and rises to her feet. Calmly, seeing clearly, she looks around. Aware of her past reality and of the need for change, she chooses her direction. She sheds the shackles that have bound her, drops them at her feet and leaves them behind as she strides majestically into a better world for herself and her loved ones. She is immense, and filled with power. So are we: powerful eternal beings filled with unlimited potential. The Maiden was asleep, bound in place by her past. She has awakened. She acts on her desire, moving forward into a better future. She is the change.

Just as it will be for you as you decide on change, the awakened Maiden is embarking on a journey. There will be dangers. She must protect herself and her loved ones. Hungry beasts will snap at her heels: wolves, fierce bears or lions that want to bring her down and destroy her. The dangers may be more subtle and take the form of others who wish her diminished or harmed. They may be her own past experiences, her thoughts, or habits. Whatever their source, these beasts, both external and internal, are real forces that must be acknowledged and dealt with. But she is prepared. She has learned how to recognize, evaluate and control them, keep them at bay or destroy them if necessary. She knows how to defend herself, to escape if needful, and how to survive and thrive.

She has never been on this road before, and the journey is not an easy one. It is long and sometimes very difficult, but she understands its importance. Her feet are sore and blistered, her muscles ache, her hands are scratched and raw, yet she continues on. She cannot see her destination clearly, but she knows she is going in the right direction by listening to her inner guide. She is forging a path through the wilderness not only for herself, but for those who will come after. Breaking the trail is hard work, and it is vitally important. She is creating and moving forward into a better future for herself and those she loves. So can you.

Here is the marvelous reality that will support you on your journey: You are a spiritual child of God, who I define as a Heavenly Father and Mother; Jesus Christ, and the Holy Spirit/Holy Ghost, all of pure perfect love, goodness and power, all fully united in purpose. For simplicity I chose to use the word He when I speak of God, although I am referring to that entire all-powerful unit. God wants us to achieve our full potential. On this earth we have a body, and a spirit which gives the body life. Our circumstances are different and our experiences and paths unique, yet God loves all of us profoundly and wants us to fulfill our destiny—here and now, and in the eternities. You are on this earth for a reason.

God tells us again and again in the holy scriptures that He wants to give us all that He has, including the fullness of His joy. We are meant to be God's heirs in the Kingdom of Heaven; this is His deepest desire for us. He will help us. May you come to understand and know this vital truth, for in it there is healing, peace, and power.

As you make your way through life there will be beautiful days filled with blue skies, birdsong and sunshine when your heart and soul will rejoice. Other days will be gloomy and cloudy, and at times there will be dark and frightening storms. Sometimes it will be *very* hard. You will meet delight, discouragement, fear, grief, pleasure and more.

Since this journey is so important why does it include misery and pain? If God loves us, why does He allow suffering? He has his reasons.

Let's explore them.

Two

What Is Suffering?

"Suffering is one of life's great teachers."
... Bryant McGill, Human Potential Thought
Leader, International Activist

Suffering is common to the entire human race. It takes many forms that will depend on our circumstances and where we are in our journey. A three-year old throwing a tantrum in the grocery store because he cannot have the red toy car he wants is miserably unhappy; anyone hearing his screams could believe he is suffering. A shy middle-schooler being taunted with 'Fatty' by peers feels painful, deep embarrassment. An executive passed over for an important promotion that seemed sure feels humiliated, angry and unappreciated. The agony of a broken leg seems unbearable. A wife or husband learning that their mate has been cheating on them feels anguish ... and on and on. The forms of human hurting are almost without end. What we can be sure of is that while we live on this earth at times we will feel pain, and sometimes life will seem exceedingly difficult.

True, as we grow physically, emotionally and spiritually we are better able to cope with the challenges that come. What embarrassed us at thirteen we can ignore at forty. We can learn to shed some things like water off a duck's back: laughing or shrugging them off as irrelevant or someone else's immaturity. But not always. Some experiences come that send us reeling, absolutely stunned by the pain or difficulty of the way. Physically, emotionally or spiritually, the suffering can be agonizing.

Here are experiences that you may relate to:

Justine shares her heartache: *"When we married we wanted to start our family immediately. Both of us loved children and wanted to have at least four. We couldn't get pregnant. Ten sad years went by, yearning for a baby, and then came the wonderful news: I was expecting a daughter! We were so excited. When she arrived we were on cloud nine! She was beautiful and we were so happy. When she was almost three months old I went in to get her one morning and found her cold in her crib. The doctors called it Sudden Infant Death Syndrome, and did not know the cause. We were devastated. How could God let such a terrible thing happen?"*

From Julie: *"My husband and I love our three children and have tried to teach them to be responsible, good people. During his last year of high school, our son turned his back on the values we taught him. He got into drugs and alcohol, he lied, he stole, and ran with a really bad crowd. We had such high hopes for him, and he just went in a completely different direction. We could see that the lifestyle he chose was leading to serious problems for him, but he would not listen to anything we said. He treated us like we were his enemy. We felt helpless. It was heartbreaking."*

Theresa's story: *"My husband Greg had worked hard with his partner to create a thriving successful business. We had a gorgeous home in an expensive neighborhood and a summer home at the beach, we sent our children to the best private schools and traveled when and where we wanted. Life was good. Then Greg began to notice some irregularities at work. As it turned out, unknown to him, his business partner had heavily invested company money in some shady dealings that quickly turned into disaster. We lost everything. We moved far away to start over. We rented a cheap apartment and my husband and I both worked at minimum wage jobs for a while. Finally, we saved enough to buy a small condo, but we are still struggling financially."*

Whatever its form, the pain can sometimes be so powerful we may wonder how we will survive it. We can lose loved ones to death, or in some other way. Suffering may come as others fail to meet our expectations. Other people make decisions that have a huge negative impact on us. Natural disasters can take everything away in a moment. Loved ones may be suffering and we feel their pain, yet are helpless to intervene. Life can unexpectedly take from us what we felt was essential for happiness.

Perhaps we experienced abuse or neglect as an innocent child or as an adult and are still suffering from its crippling effects; abuse in its varied forms can happen at any time of life and it always causes damage. Perhaps our injuries come from something more subtle: our culture, upbringing or experiences taught us that we are of little worth, that we have nothing of value to contribute, and we have come to believe it is true. Or perhaps, willfully or in ignorance, we ourselves made choices that brought suffering to us and others. And our lives can be dramatically impacted by illness or accidents.

When I was forty-five years old, my life as I knew it came to an end. I was happily raising a large family, managing our busy household and volunteering in church and community work. My youngest child was three. One spring morning I woke up feeling ill. "I've got the flu," I thought, "really *bad*." Months later I was still in bed, achingly, miserably sick, barely conscious much of the time. Usually I could not even sit up. Every part of my body hurt, including my skin, along with a profound exhaustion unlike anything I had ever experienced. It felt like a mountain had fallen on me. Even taking a few steps to the bathroom required the effort of wading through mud up to my thighs.

Several months after I became ill, I was alone in the house and very hungry; I had to have something to eat. I couldn't stand, so I crawled—a couple of feet and rested, a couple of more feet and rested—it took me half an hour to move through the short hall and down seven steps to the kitchen.

I found food, ate, and collapsed exhausted on the floor. I don't remember how I got back to bed. Some months later I thought I finally felt good enough to have dinner with the family. Holding onto walls I crept slowly down to the table, but I did not have the strength to sit upright and toppled out of the chair into a heap on the floor.

Now and then I would get a small window of respite, an hour or two, sometimes more, when the worst pain would lift and I could move and function more normally. It was hard to comprehend what had happened to me—I kept thinking, "I'll get over this soon." But I didn't. When I was able to get up and do something, functioning time was short and unpredictable. There were things that needed to be done so I tried to do them, and because I was usually at home most of the full collapses happened there. Sometimes it happened elsewhere though—at the grocery store, in a meeting, in a class, once in a huge airport parking lot. It was embarrassing, but I was so ill I didn't much care. All I could do was lie there, until eventually my body could move again.

Gradually over years I improved, until finally I felt I could go to work. With great hope I started a job, but within a week I was so ill I couldn't get out of bed. After months of recovery, I tried again. And again. And again. Even efforts at working part-time terminated in collapses that put me down for months of worsened exhaustion and misery. Later when I counted, there were twenty-three failed attempts to work.

I was either incredibly stubborn, desperate, determined, or refusing to face reality. In retrospect, all of those words fit.

Several months after I became ill, our doctor diagnosed me with what at the time was called Epstein-Barr Virus, then CFS, and then Fibro Myalgia/CFIDS. The newest term is Myalgic Encephalomyelitis, or ME/CFS and Fibro Myalgia. Our doctor recognized the illness because for a time he had worked in an office that saw many such patients. "I know what this is," he said, "But we don't know what causes it or how to treat it, except to give pain medication and tell you to rest." The resting part was easy, because most of the time that was all I could do. But since they did not learn about it in medical school and it could not be identified by conventional means, most doctors didn't believe the disease was real. Finally, now more than 30 years later, the medical community recognizes this is a serious, disabling illness. Their knowledge about it has changed little. They are still at the beginning of research, but recent work strongly suggests that the mitochondria, the energy producing part of our cells, are somehow damaged. Thus, every system in the body is impacted. Its severity ranges from rather mild to total incapacitation, and for most patients, it flares and subsides, waxes and wanes unpredictably. Other than rest and medications to treat symptoms, there is still no recognized treatment. The suicide rate for this illness is high.

I still deal with the condition. Now on a very good day I might have four hours when I can get some things done if I am careful not to overdo. Occasionally those days come two or three in a row, and that is cause for rejoicing! There are more days when 'able to be up and doing' lasts for an hour or two. Often for days in a row that thin veneer of energy is gone and all I can do is lie aching on the sofa, able only to shuffle painfully to the kitchen for simple food and back and forth to the bathroom. The energy level goes down quickly, and the lower it gets the sicker I am. Many times, I have waked up happily feeling I have the energy to go do something specific, but by the time I get ready I'm too exhausted to even get out the door, and down sick for the rest of the day. I can hold a book, and during these 'down and out of commission' times reading saves my sanity.

After the illness struck our whole world literally fell apart. My husband was fired from his job and was without work for more than a year. We lost our beautiful, spacious home in Tucson. The marriage disintegrated beyond repair and we divorced. He presented me with $45,000 of credit card debt I did not know even existed, and left the state. An attorney friend advised me my only option was bankruptcy—I was seriously ill, with children, and unable to work. A family counselor said it was crucial that I retain custody of the children for their protection, and I knew that was true. There was a small amount of child support, and spousal support for three years, which helped but barely made a dent in the need. Always looming over my shoulder was the fearful possibility that we would have to live in the car and eat out of dumpsters. I wasn't able to do much, but I did everything I could, and during those years God literally carried us in his arms, for unexpected help came from different sources when our need was extreme: the children helped as they could, our church, friends, family—somehow, we always had food to eat, a place to live, and a vehicle that ran. They were frightening, extremely difficult years. Yet I am more fortunate than many.

Christopher Reeve broke his neck when he fell from a horse, and instantly went from being Superman to a quadriplegic unable to move from his neck down. Fourteen-year-old Elizabeth Smart was kidnapped at knifepoint from her bedroom, hidden and chained to a tree, starved, abused and repeatedly raped over the following nine months until she was rescued. Natural disasters and catastrophes of war bring terrible tragedies and we watch them unfold on our TV screens. The face of suffering seems infinite in variety.

From the anguish of our souls we cry, "Why? Why this? Why me? How could God allow this to happen?" Often over time the answer becomes clear. Sometimes it does not. And still the tribulation comes. This is certain: when we pass through our own personal Gethsemane or 'The Valley of the Shadow of Death,' it will change us. What that change means is up to us. We can become angry, bitter, hurt, forever the victim of life's unfairness. Or we can allow the damaged, broken parts of us to come back together in a new, better way and choose to grow deeper, stronger and wiser. The choice is ours.

God does not cause suffering, but He allows it, and He will help us through it. Eventually, most often we can look back and with the objectivity of hindsight see that valuable lessons have been learned that perhaps could not have been learned in any other way. A wise friend told me, "When pain scoops out a hole in our heart, it creates room for compassion." It is true: such experiences give us the ability to understand and feel sorrow and empathy for others who are suffering. And, we learn truths specific to us.

I deeply believe that in the economy of God nothing is wasted—everything has a purpose. The apostle Paul in Romans 8:28, says, "And we know that all things work together for good to them that love God . . . ." Even pain and suffering. Perhaps especially pain and suffering. The truth is, it is not so much what happens to us; what matters is what we do about what comes to us. A wise man said, "All of us get broken, but some of us heal stronger in the broken places." This is our challenge.

Three

Does Suffering Have a Purpose?

"We are always in the forge or on the anvil; by trials
God is shaping us for higher things."

. . . . . . .Henry Ward Beecher

A popular saying states, "Pain is inevitable, misery is optional." It resonates, and has been attributed to many great minds who may indeed have spoken some variation of it. The recent iteration originated in a book about running by Japanese author Haruki Murakami, who attributes the saying to his brother-in-law, who was speaking primarily about—running.

Certainly it has wider application, and while I understand the intent of the statement, I differ with the inference. It would be nice if it were true, yet history shows us that suffering is a valid part of the human experience and has always been so. It is not something we always have control over, and anyone who expects to get through life without experiencing it somewhere along the way is apt to be greatly disappointed.

All of us know pain, and we will almost certainly taste suffering, whether it be physical, emotional, spiritual or mental, at some point in our life. It can be as subtle as a hidden cancer silently eating away inside, or as obvious and overwhelming as an avalanche roaring down a mountainside. It can be as swift as the sudden slice of a sword, or painfully drawn out over a long period of time. I believe it is more accurate and helpful to say, "pain is inevitable, suffering may follow. When it does, find a way to move through it somehow—don't stay stuck in the misery."

In the midst of intense pain we rarely stop to think, "Let's see now—what is the purpose of this?" A reason may become clear later; in the moment we will simply react in some instinctive way. After the initial response the important question is: how do we deal with suffering when it comes? People may become bitter and angry, striking out and railing against God and the unfair fates ever after. Some are so beaten down by the hardness of life that they stop trying and simply give up. Others attempt to escape into the temporary oblivion of alcohol, drugs, promiscuity, pornography or other addiction. There are those who seem to prefer being miserable, complaining endlessly and doing nothing to change their situation. Some people however, manage to emerge from painful experiences stronger and wiser than they were before. What makes the difference? Here, in the heat of the crucible is the critical place of decision. This is where the foundation of the future is formed. Our response to the hardship that assails us is crucial to the quality of our entire life that follows.

Some may say, "But what's the use? Life just keeps beating you down. And aren't we going to make mistakes and mess it up anyway?" Well, yes it does, and yes, we will continue to make mistakes and mess things up, sometimes terribly. And yet, human beings have the capacity to recover, to learn and grow, progress and improve. There are numerous books, articles, and qualified professional help that address this subject: the entire field of psychology and psychiatry exist for the purpose of helping people deal with life's challenges. Some helpful commonalities have emerged that are worth exploring here.

The first essential step in the journey of change is awareness. We must understand where we are in relation to where we want to be. We must be willing to deal with reality, past and present. Whatever our experience has been or is, we must see past our rationalizations and excuses for ourselves or others and acknowledge what is true and real. We cannot wisely change a situation we are not seeing clearly. And, if we have contributed to the problem in some way, we must take ownership and responsibility.

Meghan tells us: *"I was in a miserable marriage for 18 years. The best thing that came out of it was my children. My husband constantly degraded and belittled me and was often physically abusive. It didn't matter what I did, nothing pleased him. It got so bad I couldn't stand it anymore. He would not go to counseling, but finally I did. I had grown up in a similar home, and with my therapists help I came to see that when I married, it felt normal to me to be treated badly. As I got healthier I learned that I contributed to the situation in our marriage by being passive. If I wanted my life to get better, I was the one that had to change, because my husband made it clear he wasn't going to."*

Certainly Meghan didn't go into marriage expecting it to be the nightmare it became, and until she sought professional help she was unaware of how her early programming affected her choice of a partner. Very often the bad decisions we make have an unconscious foundation, and until we can make the connection, we are likely to repeat the behavior. At some point we see more clearly, and then have the choice of what we want to do about it. The importance of seeing clearly and accepting responsibility came to my awareness in an unusual way.

Every other Sunday, as a volunteer I teach two classes at our County Correctional Facility, better known as the County Jail. When I began I didn't know anyone in jail or prison, but I felt concern, and that the Personal Development life skills I'd been teaching professionally could be helpful to people who were incarcerated. I contacted the appropriate person and asked. I wasn't credentialed to teach in their system so he referred me to a spiritual leader in the community. They did need someone to teach a class on Sundays to women inmates.

From my own experience I knew how helpful, indeed crucial, spirituality has been to me, and so I accepted that opportunity. It has turned out to be one of the richest experiences of my life.

I had never been to a prison or jail, and the first time I went I was amazed at the sheer size of the place; it held just under 1,000 inmates. It was functional, the opposite of luxurious, but clean and well maintained. It was however, definitely a jail. All volunteers must pass an intensive background check and are well trained before permitted any contact with inmates. There are strict rules, including how we interact with inmates, and what we can bring in—almost nothing. The rules define virtually everything about being there, and they are in place for good reasons.

To get to the classrooms the fifteen or so Sunday instructors, men and women, go through a thick steel door that buzzes harshly open and clangs shut behind, locking us into a small closed space for what feels like a long minute. Then the matching door a few feet away buzzes open and we move into a larger space where several guards are manning monitors. As we file past they check our authorization and what we bring with us. We move through another space with guards and a bigger, stronger steel door into the interior of the jail itself.

Each week we have a short prayer meeting in the miniature chapel and then wait in our various assigned classrooms while a guard announces to the cell blocks (called pods) that church services are being held. The inmates who want to come, line up and are escorted to the classroom by a guard who remains outside in the hall. When the classroom steel doors shut we are locked in; the doors do not open from the inside. Each classroom has a hand-held alarm with a big red button that we are to use if anything begins to get dicey. Attendance ranges from thirty inmates to two—we never know until they file in.

There are many more men than women in the facility, and sexes are kept strictly segregated. People in jail are waiting for bail to be posted or for their court date, which will determine whether they stay longer, are released, or sentenced to move into the state prison. They are there for days, weeks or months, rarely as long as a year. In our jail most inmates are white, with a sprinkling of people of color. Many women rotate through. They are a mix of scared, angry, defiant and hopeless, locked away from friends, family, and freedom. This Sunday class is a safe place to express emotions, and while we never ask such questions, women often open up and talk about their damaged lives. Their stories are sobering, sad, and sometimes tragic. Somewhere along the line choices were made that have borne bitter fruit.

Even so, surprisingly, there is a marvelous spirit felt during the classes. It is something I had not expected. Occasionally class members are restless or hostile when they file in, but as the lesson progresses they quiet and I feel their full attention as the room is permeated with a beautiful spirit of love. It comes from God, and it happens every Sunday.

As teachers we have no lesson manual, and as I prepare, my prayers are that I can teach these women what God wants them to hear. The subjects vary widely, but one underlying theme comes through clearly every week and undergirds everything: "Teach them that I love them. They need to know that I love them."

My job is to be an instrument in God's hands and I do the best I can, hoping the Spirit will penetrate hardened and hurting hearts. It is an extraordinary experience, week after week. A choice for a new way of seeing and being is opened to them if they are willing. When they are, God touches hearts in a tender, beautiful and powerful way. When that happens you can see and hear it—their voices change, and understanding and hope blossom in their face and eyes. Often there are tears. Sometimes lives are changed.

There are many reasons these women are there; after they are released, staying out of jail is the challenge. It usually requires major life changes. Some are able to make the necessary transitions and some are not. In talking with guards and other teachers more experienced than I, it is clear that a sticking point for many inmates is taking responsibility for their own part in their incarceration—often in their minds, the reason they are there is someone or something else's fault. As long as they continue to blame only others, they are stuck in a cycle that with variations of situation and actors, repeats itself over and over again. Many have been there three or six or ten times before.

Without question, life can be horrifically unfair, and many of these women have been dealt a hard hand. Nearly all have experienced abuse of some kind. In the jail and prison population addiction to drugs, alcohol, or other harmful activities plays a major role. And mental illness can be a factor.

While most people who experience abuse and the trauma it can cause do not make choices that lead to incarceration, research shows that there can be a connection. In his pioneering landmark work *The Body Keeps the Score*, Dr. Bessel van der Kolk, his team and others researching the field, report that brain imaging confirms that trauma is far more pervasive than formerly thought. Trauma literally changes the way the brain functions and reacts, often at levels beyond conscious awareness. This is especially true when it happens in childhood while the brain is still forming. The more negative factors that enter in and the more severe the trauma, the more likelihood there is for the development of serious, ongoing problems that carry into adulthood.

It seems obvious that as a society we would have better results if we focused more on healing deep damage at the root, rather than trying to suppress the symptoms that manifest from it. That, however, requires societal change beyond the scope of this book. In the meantime, we work with what we have and what we know. There are many factors of course, and each woman's story is different. But in the end, all are the product of environment and conscious and unconscious choices that set a trajectory. Sometimes inmates connect being in jail to their choices, often they do not.

It is only when they acknowledge the truths of their lives and the part they play in it, either as an active or passive participant, that positive change can happen. They have to see clearly, desire something better, accept responsibility for what they can control, believe it is possible, commit, and actively take steps toward improvement. It can be very challenging, for it means making drastic changes, internal and external. There are programs set up for the specific purpose of helping inmates both inside the jail and after their release that offer excellent resources and are sorely needed. But they don't and can't solve everything. Even with the best support, in the end it is up to the individual.

Occasionally in class the inmates teach each other, and some have figured it out: "Guys," Krystal said recently, "If we don't want to keep coming back here, we have to take the responsibility. It doesn't do any good to be mad at everybody else. Every one of us did something that got us here, and we're the ones who have to change it."

So it is with all of us whatever our own situation. It seems sometimes that we almost 'sleepwalk' through our lives—moving along with little awareness. Yet aware or unaware, choices are made, and choices have consequences. If something in our lives is causing trouble, we are the ones who have to acknowledge the problem and make changes. Staring hard reality in the face is uncomfortable at the least, and can be truly painful. It requires courage.

When faced with a difficult situation our first response may be that someone else needs to change and the problem will be solved. Perhaps it would help, but that is a road that leads nowhere, because as much as we may want to, we cannot force someone else to change. We can try—we can teach and persuade and attempt to convince, but ultimately the only person we can ever really control is ourselves. If we want things to be different in our lives, we must take responsibility for bringing about the changes we desire. Yes, it will be challenging, and perhaps extremely difficult. But there is no surer way to fail than to never try. You are a being of profound potential, and you can do hard things. You will find that you are stronger than you know.

Sometimes we are at the mercy of forces beyond our control—fire, flood, crime, hurricanes or tornadoes, illness, war, drought or earthquake. Even in the midst of disaster there still remains an element of choice in our response. When life hits us hard, it hurts. We are stunned, deeply upset, depressed, or any of a thousand other devastating emotions. We are human beings with powerful feelings which need to be acknowledged. An essential part of dealing with reality is to allow ourselves to feel what we feel. Trying to ignore the pain, pretending it did not happen or does not matter, hinders healing. To heal we need to recognize, acknowledge and experience the emotion. Name it and feel it! Then, and this is crucial, if it is negative, move through it. Staying stuck in anger or hurt or bitterness will only reinforce the negativity.

Don't let the blackbird of unhappiness build a permanent nest in your heart. When the time is right, gently, firmly shoo the dark-feathered fellow away, realizing that he will call back occasionally and that is all right—he will come and he will go, and you will be able to deal with it. Deep grief that rends into our very soul is a different experience; recovery from that kind of wound takes longer. Even then, it is possible. Grief counseling can help. For myself and many others, deep healing comes from God and the profound love, comfort and solace He offers. It can take time—perhaps years, but the pain does soften, and while the sorrow may never go completely away, we learn to tuck it into a corner of our heart and feel able and positive again.

The experience of suffering is universal, but finding our way out of it is a very individual matter. There are no rules about how long we are allowed to hurt, or exactly how to navigate through grief and pain. It takes as long as it takes for you. We just must be sure that while unhappiness is part of the journey, it is not the destination. Talking to a trusted friend, counseling and prayer can all help, as does time. Long-lasting severe depression requires professional help.

In the midst of our pain we are prone to cry out, "Why? Why would God allow such a terrible thing to happen?" Three reasons come to my mind.

First: God has given human beings their free will or agency on this earth. Whatever the source of pain in our lives, we get to make choices about our response, and consequences follow. In this way we learn what brings joy or what brings sorrow. We learn to look beneath the surface and come to better recognize the difference between truth and error before we step into it. We learn that while some choices may bring temporary pleasure—a new car or boat or house we can't really afford; a hot fudge sundae every Friday and Monday, with doughnuts, french fries and Kit Kats in between; a 'harmless' flirtation with your spouse's best friend or that interesting person at the office; drugs, gambling or pornography for their high, or alcohol for its 'buzz' and numbing ability—the costs can steal health, peace of mind, and real, lasting happiness.

We can learn, mindfully choose well and enjoy the benefits that accompany good decisions, or we can be thoughtlessly passive and let someone or something else determine the course of our life. We can close our eyes to reality and pretend that all is well while our lives quietly crumble to pieces around us. Or decide it's just too much trouble to try to change, and continue living far below our potential. We could willfully insist that we should always have things our way—if we want something then certainly we should have it, heedless of the cost to others. We can do so, but this is a path which often leads to a sad harvest: we may reach out and grab what we want and find it turns into the sawdust of disappointment trickling through our fingers.

So many choices! How are we to know what is best? This is after all, not a dress rehearsal; it is real life with real consequences. Certainly God knows what is best, and yet with all His power He never forces us. The power of decision is in our own hands—we get to choose. And because we are developing, growing, imperfect beings, sometimes our choices will be good and sometimes they will not; sometimes they will bring joy, sometimes sorrow. Other people's choices may harm us. How unfair that is! Yes, it is, and God allows even that to happen, because this is a test for everyone—both the caring and the cruel. It is an opportunity for each of us to demonstrate who we really are.

Will we take responsibility for the trajectory of our own life, whatever the hand we are dealt? Can we learn to be considerate, responsible and unselfish, or will we be demanding, self-centered and willing to hurt others to get what we want? Will we come through tribulation embittered, or be made deeper and wiser by it? Even when we are the victim of circumstance or of someone else's poor decisions, we can choose to become stronger from the experience. The choices we make over time define who we are. Who will we become from what life brings to us?

A second reason God allows trials and tribulation is because it is the best possible pathway for us to become the powerful, wise and loving beings we are meant to be. Each of us have qualities and abilities to offer that are uniquely ours; we are all needed. God already knows who we are meant to be, we are given the opportunity to learn it for ourselves. Painful as it may be, opposition is necessary for growth, and from it, essential life lessons can come that are not gained by any other means. Many significant far-reaching causes that have improved the world began as a result of individual suffering.

A father who lost his young son to a murder that was never solved developed and hosted the top-rated television program "America's Most Wanted," and over 1,000 dangerous criminals were apprehended as a result. John Walsh, the show's creator, continues to advocate for victims of crimes. A mother in Oklahoma whose son committed suicide began an online support community that now brings comfort and information to hundreds of thousands of grieving families worldwide. A young mother who suffered terrible disfiguring burns in an airplane crash started a blog that has brought daily inspiration to millions. Corrie Ten Boom and Victor Frankl survived the horrors of the Nazi concentration camps of World War II. They did not know each other, but both found a resilience that transcended the experience and became human beings who have blessed the lives of tens of millions of people all over the world with their wisdom. Every one of us can look around and see people to admire who are what they are because of things they overcame.

The analogy of the trees is true: One tree stood in an exposed, stony field where it had to sink its roots deep to find water and nourishment and anchor against the blowing wind. Another grew in a protected place where water and nourishment was plentiful. It had no need to struggle or sink deep roots. When a fierce storm came the tree with strong limbs and deep roots survived. The other tree, with its easy life and shallow roots was torn from the ground and died.

So it is for us. Just as a strong body requires exertion to maintain strength, so must we also experience opposition to gain strength of character. If life is too easy it is human nature to begin to take it all for granted and become apathetic and weak. Our personal strength of character is often forged in the furnace of adversity.

I believe the third reason God allows suffering is because He wants us to come to know Him. Most of us are accustomed to depending upon our own toughness to get us through difficult times, and often it will. There are times though, when even more is required. In desperation we may turn to friends and family for understanding and help, yet sometimes even they fail us. When our world comes crashing down around our ears and the problem is bigger than we or human effort can fix, then it is that we often turn to God. Our suffering tenderizes and enlarges our heart and sometimes breaks it wide open, raw and bleeding.

At the height and depth of these heart-wrenching times God will support us when we turn to Him. I know this personally. At one point in my life when I felt I could bear no more, I fell to my knees and in anguish cried out, "Where are you, God?" The answer was immediate. "I am here, Linda, beside you." And He was. I felt Him there next to me, and I was encompassed in the strength of His love, His compassion, and His powerful, never ending support. He bore me up then as He had before and does still to this day. In my extremity I have come to know Him. He loves you in the same way, and He is there for us, ever ready when we turn to Him.

The Holy Bible likens human suffering to the refiner's fire in which metal-bearing ore is thrust into a fire so intensely hot that it destroys the dross rock and leaves only pure gold. If we choose, we can emerge from the darkness of loss and suffering and the fire of adversity improved—stronger and wiser, with increased capacity and deepened compassion, more fit to help and serve and make a positive difference.

Quite naturally, we do not like for things to be hard; we resist and rebel against it. And yet, Alfred Adler, a psychologist and father of Individual and Community Psychology, determined after much study and observation, "Overcoming difficulties leads to courage, self-respect, and knowing yourself." Kahlil Gibran in his book *The Prophet,* noted, "Out of suffering have emerged the strongest souls." It is in overcoming difficulties that we learn how strong we are.

What is the purpose of adversity? Why, if God loves us, does he allow us to suffer? Because He gives us free will to make choices and to learn from their consequences. Because in doing so we are improved, and we become wiser, deeper and more able. Because if we let it, suffering strengthens us. And God needs strong men and women to help heal this hurting world.

That is why.

Four

Dysfunctional, You Say?

*". . . I believe that this neglected, wounded inner child
of the past is the major source of human misery."*

. . . . . John Bradshaw, psychologist

The psychologist, John Bradshaw quoted above, cites research that found 96% of all families to be to some degree 'dysfunctional'—meaning the system by which the family interacts is distorted in such a way that family members are negatively impacted. "Most people think they come from a dysfunctional family," says Dr. Michael Kerr, a psychiatrist at Georgetown University Family Center.

Goodness knows my children did. I remember looking at my firstborn nestled in my arms, the wonder and love I felt, and wanting with my whole being to be a perfect mother for this precious child. As each child came, I felt the same. But of course, I wasn't a perfect mother. Even though I love my children heart and soul and was doing the very best I knew how, I still made mistakes. Parenting brings joys like nothing else and it is worth every bit of effort, but it is not an easy job and we are imperfect human beings. While most people want to be good mothers and fathers and do the best they can, our intentions sometimes don't match up with our knowledge and ability. Without question, a strong healthy family is the best possible place to learn the attitudes and skills that prepare us for life. It is also a laboratory in which all the participants are learning.

Hopefully as children we were fortunate enough to experience much that was positive in a nurturing, supportive atmosphere. Yet just as every human being grapples with their individual challenges, so too do families. The positive or negative impact is profound, not only on individuals but on society. The need to know how to relate wisely and well to others and to ourselves, and how to deal with the challenges of existence determines everyone's happiness and success in life. Despite all our progress in science and technology, human relations continue to be an unconquered frontier—people still struggle along, suffering and causing suffering, as they have done as far back as history is recorded.

Inevitably, we are all the products of our family or absence of family. Some of us will be parents and some will not, but everyone impacts those around us. And even though some families experience problems so severe that children must be removed from the home to have a chance at thriving, most manage to do quite a lot of things right. Despite their various and unique challenges, families remain the best structure for the nurturing and training of human beings, giving both children and parents opportunity for growth, learning, and the essential connection and love that is a basic human need. There is nothing that can replace a family whose members love and support each other.

While we all have our big or little hang-ups that affect how we interact with others, in some families the problems are so severe that they produce children who grow into adults who are truly damaged or emotionally crippled. The defining factor of dysfunctionality is the severity of the problems. Depending upon the circumstances and people involved, the consequences of dysfunction can range from minor to disastrous.

In the individual, most experts would agree that the negative effects of being raised in a dysfunctional family can include:

- Low self-esteem and insecurity
- Lack of trust in others
- Incorrect beliefs
- Disabling shame/inappropriate guilt
- Chronic anxiety
- Fear of risks/failure/success
- Inappropriate or poorly defined boundaries
- Impaired ability to form healthy relationships

One result is divorce. In 2018, statistics say that the probability of divorce in the U.S. is 40 to 50% for every marriage that occurs, and that 28% of children under the age of 18 live in single parent homes. I am part of that demographic.

I was a mother with our four youngest children at home when I divorced my husband of 27 years. Like most people, when I married, I made my decision based on what I knew at the time; I loved my husband and looked forward to a long, mutually supportive life together. The marriage turned out to be one of mental, emotional, financial, verbal and occasional physical abuse. A psychologist who knew my husband described him as "A master of psychological warfare." And because of my own dysfunction I was slow to recognize the abuse for what it was. The children also suffered as a result of all this.

Even given the extreme hardship of the following years, I never regretted the divorce. Was I sad because it was necessary? Yes, absolutely. One hopes that when problems arise in marriage as they inevitably will, both partners will learn better ways to function and difficulties can be worked out. For a variety of reasons it isn't always possible. Even so, from that marriage came my children, a blessing I would not have missed for anything.

After many years I married again. The marriage commenced in great love and concluded in heartache by circumstances beyond anyone's control. For that experience there is no regret, only appreciation for tasting how good and sweet marriage can be, for the growth it precipitated, and love that continues.

As my first marriage disintegrated, I gradually came to understand that as a result of experiences during my childhood years and my own personality, I had a distorted view of my place and rights in a family. I was born during World War II in Los Angeles, California, eight months after 360 Japanese warplanes swarmed out of the sky and attacked Pearl Harbor, Hawaii, destroying much of the U.S. Naval fleet and taking thousands of U.S. lives. The next day we were at war with Japan and within three days, also with Italy and Germany. The war, of course, dominated everything.

Some say that our earliest memories are possible only because someone told us of them. That is not always true. I never heard my family talk about any of these experiences, but although I was only a toddler, my memories of wartime Los Angeles are vividly clear. I remember occasionally feeling fear in the adults around me. On nights when the siren wailed, we pulled down blackout curtains in our homes and vehicles pulled over and turned off their lights and engines. The whole teeming city went dark and hushed as dozens of huge columns of light thrust up, prowling the black skies, searching for enemy aircraft. One day our family including aunts, uncles and cousins, went outside and faced inland. We first heard then felt an increasing deep rumbling, and suddenly coming up over the horizon the whole sky filled with airplanes roaring low overhead, what seemed like endless rows of them, thousands of planes heading off to war in the Pacific.

My father joined the Navy before my first birthday and returned when I was three years and three months old. About 16 months later a little brother came along, followed by more children. I don't know what my sibling's experiences were, but with one exception, my earliest memories of my father are of his hurting me, and his rage, jerking me about and spanking me hard. It happened often, and I never knew what I had done to make him angry. Expressing needs, wants, or unhappiness was punished by one or both parents, and mentioning and enjoying accomplishments also met with harsh disapproval, especially from my mother. It seemed to me that whatever I was feeling or thinking, my parents absolutely did not want to know about it. They did not express approval or affection verbally or physically, and what I learned without knowing I was learning it, was that in the family, feelings were unacceptable. I unconsciously coped by burying what I felt so deep I usually didn't realize it was there. Outside the family I was generally confident and cheerful, I had friends I enjoyed and who enjoyed me—but with my parents, it was different. It took me a long time to figure it all out.

Looking back, I have some understanding. My mother and father were people with many admirable qualities. They were responsible, capable and sociable, they gladly served in our community and church, everyone knew they loved each other, and both of them worked very hard to provide for their family. They were good examples in many ways. I feel they were doing the best they knew. But there was a serious deficit when it came to dealing with emotions. I believe they simply didn't know how. They grew up in a different world. Their grandparents and parents were those that faced the wilderness and settled the frontier. Diphtheria, smallpox, scarlet fever and other deadly illnesses were common, and just after the turn of the century, World War I and the Spanish Flu added to the toll. Life was hard, and mostly about survival.

During their childhood my parents experienced the Great Depression. There was no government aid to help and they and their families suffered, often lacking food and other necessities. As the Depression ended World War II began. As young adults they were required to fight the crushing war machines of the Axis Powers and their threat of world domination. The men went off to war in Europe or the South Pacific and those at home did everything they could to support them. The times placed huge demands on them, and I believe they simply could not allow themselves to pay attention to how they felt. "What you want or feel means nothing, just do what you are supposed to do," enabled them to keep functioning. Quite naturally, they passed this same viewpoint along in their parenting.

It impacted me at a foundational level. I wanted to please my parents, as children do, and I remember acutely feeling I was doing something seriously, morally wrong if I needed something, or felt unhappy about anything. In my unconscious belief system, no matter what happened I was to put up with it and always keep smiling. I know now that this is unrealistic and extremely unhealthy. But unaware, I carried this concept into adulthood, with predictable consequences. Eventually the misery backed up like too much water behind a dam, until finally it was unbearable.

Slowly, painfully I came to see the reality of the dysfunctional patterns in our marriage and my own skewed thinking, and began learning how to think, feel and act in healthier ways. Over time it became absolutely clear that I was the only partner interested in making any positive changes.

Of course, all of this deeply affected the children. Despite the family dynamic they grew up in, they have shown amazing resilience. Each is an accomplished, compassionate, uniquely engaging adult, each of them making a positive difference in their own individual way. It has not been easy—they have all faced serious life challenges, which they are handling with strength and wisdom. They are remarkable men and women.

Because of my own experience with marriage I take exception to the way the problem of broken families is often discussed, with the villain usually being 'Divorce'. I suppose there are divorces that are frivolous and unnecessary, but those I know who have divorced made the decision only after serious efforts to salvage the relationship, deep soul searching, and heartache. Divorce is not the problem—divorce is the visible result that indicates a deeper problem.

The problem is rooted in dysfunctional attitudes and beliefs that determine how we view ourselves, interact with others, and handle the stresses of life. Most often these patterns go directly back to the childhood that shaped us. Usually people are doing the best they can with what they know, but that does not change the fact that many attitudes and behaviors are problematic, and until we become aware we blindly repeat what is familiar, and wonder why life isn't working the way we want.

While families struggle for different reasons, often they don't know how to function in any other way, and so fail to nurture and support the healthy emotional growth of children in important ways. Some do not provide even the essentials of a safe physical environment. The effect on children, who grow into adults, is serious. Dysfunctional patterns, whatever their severity, are likely to repeat from one generation to another, with individuals, families, and society feeling the unhappy results.

The good news is that there is hope. Rather than heedlessly repeating what is familiar, as adults we have the opportunity and responsibility to evaluate and make changes. Healthier more positive and productive ways can be learned and implemented. My own awakening came slowly. I hope yours will come sooner and less painfully. Wherever you are on your path, whatever you want to improve, gaining new knowledge from good sources and acting upon it can help you in a powerful way. People can change if they choose. Families can improve the way they interact with each other. Helpful, solid information is now available to anyone who seeks it—with a desire to learn and appropriate help and tools, we can make changes for the better.

The process of positive growth generates tremendous satisfaction, opening whole new worlds of understanding and opportunity. It does require courage and real effort, and may initially be uncomfortable or even painful. And, change is not always welcome—some people are willing to experience this type of growth and some are not. Either choice has predictable results: the fact remains that when we consciously or unconsciously do not acknowledge negative patterns or qualities, we can be quite sure that we will continue to have to deal with whatever unpleasant consequences follow. Paraphrasing Stephen R. Covey: "We can choose our actions (or inaction), but we cannot choose the consequences of those actions." We do reap what we sow, even when we sow in ignorance.

Through the ages of history humankind has grappled with similar challenges. Although the first known discussions about how to live effectively are thousands of years old, the formal study of human behavior as a science is recent. The development of the Social Sciences is a fascinating evolution.

In about 400 B.C. in Ancient Greece, philosopher Socrates theorized about life. He considered dialogue more effective than writing, so it was his followers that made a written record of his ideas, in some of the earliest documents of the impact of an outspoken, influential wise man. Simplifying, Socrates said that people should think for themselves and do what was right because it was right, regardless of prevailing opinion. He was admired by daring free thinkers; by the authorities he was imprisoned and forced to drink poisonous hemlock for teaching heretical ideas to the young men of Athens.

At the midpoint of human history Jesus Christ lived in Judea under Roman rule. Against prevailing ideology, he taught his revolutionary gospel of love, saying the two greatest commandments were to love God and to love one's neighbor as oneself, caring for each other and forgiving and praying for enemies. He taught, he healed, and he worked miracles. Thousands of people flocked after him. Considered a threat to the power of the local leaders he lived among, he was crucified on a cross, where he died. As he had said he would, three days later he rose from the tomb, and interacted with hundreds of people over the following days. His three short years of ministry impacted the world like nothing else before or since; thousands of years later he continues to be the lodestone for billions of people all over the world. The truths he taught continue to be rediscovered.

While there were notable thinkers in the span of years between—Goethe stands out—a noticeable change began emerging in the Mid-Nineteenth Century. American philosopher William James shook the status quo by announcing, "The greatest discovery of my generation is that a human being can alter his life by altering his attitudes." James was suggesting that change on all levels of being was possible, both internal and external. Now recognized as the father of American Psychology, William James changed the trajectory of prevailing thought about human development.

The climate was ripe for new ideas. Near the same time Alfred Adler, the father of Individual Psychology, was a student of Sigmund Freud in Austria. He later broke with Freud, coming to different conclusions. Adler observed that human beings have a driving, built-in desire to fulfill their potential, and from his studies determined that experiences in the early years have a great impact on the development of human personality. He stated that many problems can be avoided by treating children with respect and awareness of their needs. This was revolutionary thinking in the culture of the early 1800's when children were traditionally seen as small, often naughty adults, and punishment, frequently severe, was the normally accepted way of 'training' them.

These new thinkers broke the ground, and others have built upon their work. Victor Frankl, a psychotherapist in Vienna, Austria in the mid-twentieth century survived incarceration at Auschwitz, one of the World War II Nazi death camps. In this harsh, inhumane setting he further formulated his theories and later authored *Man's Search for Meaning*. He is most famous for saying, "Everything can be taken from a man but one thing: to choose one's attitude in any given set of circumstances." And for stating, "The salvation of man is through love." His book had a tremendous impact; after the shattering devastation of two closely set world wars people were ready to consider human behavior in new ways.

Gradually, information about the new field of Human Behavioral Sciences began to filter into the public consciousness. In 1964 psychiatrist Eric Berne authored the best selling *Games People Play,* followed by Dr. Thomas A. Harris with the hugely popular book *I'm OK, You're OK.* Additional specialists in the field followed, including John Bradshaw's *Healing the Shame That Binds You.* Soon more best-selling books appeared to help individuals understand and heal themselves and relationships. And they continue to come. Many valuable contributions to the complex body of knowledge about human behavior are available and the field continues to evolve.

Without question, a good beginning in an emotionally healthy home gives tremendous lifelong advantages. However, even when elements of a 'good home' are lacking, some still find their way to emotional stability. Despite an appalling early environment of parental alcoholism, addiction, abuse or neglect, there are those who rise above their circumstances and create a positive, productive life. These individuals are inspiring. On the other hand, some with every apparent advantage choose a path harmful to themselves or others. Choices are made, and every human being bears the consequences of their own. Most of us trudge along somewhere in the middle, toting our individual bags of mixed beliefs, positive and negative, accurate and inaccurate. If we're lucky we arrive at adulthood with strengths and a healthy respect for both ourselves and others. Frequently however, by the time childhood is over, many of us are shaped in ways that hinder us to some degree or another. We can choose to do something about it. As adults, our responsibility is to educate ourselves and make the changes we deem necessary.

We all come into this world knowing how important we are—babies and toddlers are brimming with energetic confidence. A foundational challenge is to help them find the balance between their needs and wants and those of others. Too often in that molding process children come to believe either that what they think or want is all that matters, or that their needs or desires are not important to anyone including themselves. Both are harmful paradigms that cause problems in the ability to successfully navigate the challenges of life. Emotional health lies in a balance between the two.

The fact that false beliefs and seriously dysfunctional human relationships can distort the way we see the world without us even recognizing their impact is illustrated by the following experiences:

From Allison: *"I grew up the youngest child of four older brothers. They were often mean to me. They were bigger and stronger and made sure I knew they were also smarter. As far as they were concerned I was weak and stupid and basically worthless. My parents either didn't notice their treatment of me or didn't feel it mattered, but eventually I came to believe it was true. My brothers continued to bully and try to control me even as an adult, expecting me to submit to their supposed superiority. And usually I did.*

I was forty before I finally began to realize that I am actually an intelligent person with real skills, and capable of making good choices for myself. I lost a lot of years before I realized I could be in charge of my life. My brothers still haven't changed, but I have. They don't like the new me, but honestly, I don't care. I am finally learning who I am and what I can do, and I like it!"

The impact of the early years plays out in many ways: an abused child might learn to view the world as a place where no one can be trusted and everyone is out to harm them. Others learn that the way to solve problems is to be angry, yell and hurt people, or to function in an indirectly hostile passive-aggressive way, such as presenting a friendly face while bad-mouthing and spreading vicious gossip about someone behind their back. An overindulged child may learn selfishness, arrogance and/or cruelty. A neglected child may believe that they deserve nothing, their needs don't matter and neither do they. Another may learn that the best way to get what they want is to be manipulative, devious, or to lie. The variations are endless. For these and others, unless a more effective way is learned, there is bound to be a rocky road ahead as far as relationships are concerned.

Jennifer, 36, shares her experience: *"I am an only child, and my parents were extremely indulgent and over permissive. As a*

*child I had few friends; after once or twice children didn't want
to play with me. As an adult I still have serious problems with
relationships both personally and at work. I suppose my parents
thought they were being loving, but I have a lot of resentment
toward them for not teaching me how to consider other people's
needs and feelings, or how to function in a world where I don't
always get my own way. It has been so hard I am now in counseling, trying to catch up on things I should have been taught a
long time ago."*

Just like putting on a pair of colored eyeglasses, whatever
we learn in those early years becomes the lens through which
we view the world. Until we come to an awareness of our
negative programming it will impact how we function, and
we will carry it into our adult lives with its consequences—
our attitudes and behavior directed by an autopilot pointed
in a faulty direction. Very often we simply don't recognize the
problem until something forcefully brings it to our attention.
A few years ago this was brought home to me in a way that
made me chuckle when I figured it out.

As I was getting dressed to go to a meeting, I realized
that I was feeling anxious. It was somewhere I wanted to go
and I had plenty of time; there was no reason to feel anxiety,
but I did. I thought, "I never realized it before, but I always
feel anxious when I'm getting ready to go out. Hm. Why is
that?" It didn't take long to figure out the probable roots: my
mother insisted our family arrive at least twenty minutes early
to everything. For as long as I can remember she was strongly

pressuring me to 'hurry up' when we went out. Possibly delaying was an unconscious way of my young self to resist being pressured, or perhaps I was a natural dawdler. Either or both, the result was that for years I was in the habit of being late. I didn't like it and didn't really understand why I was always late, it just kept happening.

It was a relatively small problem (at least for me!) and I worked around it. That changed when I became an airline stewardess (now called a flight attendant) and recognized that if I wanted to keep my job, being late for a flight was not an option. I immediately developed the habit of being on time for flights, and it wasn't long before being on time for everything became my new normal. But because I was so good at ignoring my feelings, the anxiety when getting ready to go out remained unnoticed for many years.

When I finally recognized what I was experiencing and figured out its roots, I was able to easily manage it. As anxiety reared its niggly little head I would say to myself, "Oh, you're feeling anxious. You know where that comes from—it's 'old stuff' that does not apply to now. No one is pressuring you; there's no reason to feel this way. Just blow that away, like a piece of fluff. There. It's gone." And because that approach was accurate, it was. The significant point is that the negative emotion remained in place invisible to me until I really paid attention to what I was feeling and figured out its source. This happened to be a rather small issue that I could laugh about, but some are much weightier, with more serious consequences.

Many people can relate to experiences like the one Elise shares: *"My parents provided a home, food and clothes, but they did not express love or approval in any other way, either physical or verbal. I learned very early that I would be furiously spanked if I wanted something or cried about anything. I felt my father actively disliked me and my mother merely tolerated me. Sarcasm and bullying was the norm in the extended family. My way of handling it all was to bury negative feelings so deeply that most of the time even I didn't know they were there. It was not conscious. I understand now that it was a way of coping that allowed me to survive my childhood with less trauma.*

However, this has caused serious problems for me as an adult, especially in relationships with men. I did not know how to pay attention to my feelings, and didn't recognize red flags or danger signals in relationships. I thought ignoring my needs and being treated badly was simply normal. I've been in and out of three abusive marriages. I'm only now beginning to figure all this out."

Elements of Elise's story resonate with me. Often it is pain that finally brings us to the point of trying to 'figure it out.' If it is uncomfortable enough we ask ourselves, "Why did this happen, and why does it keep happening? What am I doing wrong, or what don't I know that I need to know?" Then we are at the point of readiness to learn. Until then we are likely to continue following the deeply worn pathways of distorted perceptions and unhealthy responses, suffering the misery they can bring and puzzled as to why.

There are other subtle ways to sabotage ourselves. In her book titled *Spiritual Lightening,* M. Catherine Thomas points out, "The past wants to hold us prisoner as we obsess over mistakes and other sources of pain." It is true. Sometimes, just as our tongue keeps probing an aching tooth, we keep activating a remembered emotional injury over and over rather than dealing with it. The painful tooth brings a problem to our attention; if we are wise we will call the dentist for an appointment. Emotional distress is just as real and important, but easier to ignore—without realizing it we may obsessively go back in our thoughts and feelings to past sources of injustice, pain or shame, reliving them again and again, deepening the neural pathways without ever addressing the problem. This habit is so invisible that the mindset becomes our default setting. The feeling of resentment, anger, hurt or guilt is so familiar that we don't even realize it is there—unconsciously believing it is a natural extension of ourselves. It is not. It is in fact, harmful.

These negative pathways and the emotions they produce are part of the human experience born of bullying, ridicule, trauma, neglect, manipulation, shame, physical, mental, sexual and emotional abuse, and our own mistakes. Untreated, they prevent people from thriving. They require being acknowledged, and examined with clear eyes so we can decide what to do with them. If they are not serving us in a positive way we can choose to consciously correct them. Occasionally in this process we may find that our painful interpretation of an experience is based on misinformation or misunderstanding.

Sometimes hurt is intentionally inflicted. Abuse, with all its ugly faces, is always a product of dysfunction. It harms the mind and spirit and often injures the body as well. Abuse in every form leaves scars that can disable. Often these traumas and wounds are invisible to the eye, yet manifest in dysfunctional human relationships or faulty self care. The perpetrators may accept responsibility for what they did, or they may not.

While we may have good reason to feel wounded, enraged and bitter, we can still choose to heal. Blaming our parents, spouse, or someone else initially may be grounded in fact, but we do not have to continue on that course. Regardless of the circumstances across the whole range of injuries from minor to severe, in the end we are the ones, the only ones, who can be responsible for our own healing.

Yes, it is absolutely important to say what is true. Justifying or trying to cover up or ignore abuse is never the answer. Damage needs to be acknowledged, feelings felt, named and respected, and corrections made as possible. We need to protect ourselves in whatever lawful way is effective. Nevertheless, nourishing hate and revenge is counterproductive to recovery. By staying in that dark place we are the ones who are most damaged, and we give the abuser power to continue hurting us.

We can mindfully choose to move beyond the effects of abuse or neglect. A large body of useful self-help literature now exists both in print and online, and knowledgeable professionals are specifically trained to help in this process. We discount it at our peril: if we choose to ignore the information available about dysfunction in family systems and human interaction we can put the wellbeing of ourselves, our children, and others at risk. Be open to learning, and listen to your own inner guide.

As people interact with one another, everyone to some extent or another will deal with dysfunctional relationships. We can come to recognize toxic situations for what they are and learn how to protect ourselves and confidently deal with them. Whatever the source of our wounds, whatever their severity, as we identify the unhealthy patterns in our lives we shift into a position from which we can begin the process of healing. Wherever we are, that is where we begin. Positive, hopeful, productive perspectives and actions can replace negatives and become an automatic part of us. Old harmful ways can be left behind to disturb us no more. Just as our allegorical Sleeping Maiden has done, we must rise up and take charge of our lives.

For many the strength to implement change and healing is tremendously increased by including their Higher Power in the process. In spite of abuse, in spite of neglect, despite our own errors, regardless of the depth of the damage, the deep reality we need to understand is this: Inside each of us is a flawless, perfectly loved magnificent daughter or son of the living God, with the potential for great power and great good. This is who we really are. Rarely do we see ourselves in this way, perhaps most of us never do because we have learned to see ourselves as less, far less. Yet each of us carry within a spark of divine fire waiting to be ignited. Beginning very early, life can beat us down and temporarily dim that essential glowing ember. But it remains, and if we nurture it, the innate drive to become greater than we are will continue to glow brighter and brighter—we rightfully desire to rise into the intelligent, powerful beings we were created to become. The universe and God Himself desires it for us.

Becoming aware offers the opportunity for improvement. We need not remain a victim of dysfunctional patterning in our past, instead we can use it as a springboard to growth. We can reclaim our own innate power and recover from past wounds and trauma. Always, God's unlimited love and resources are available to us when we ask for His help. As we learn more effective ways to think, to be, and to interact with the world, our understanding, strength and happiness increase. Our mind and heart begin to open to the sun like the unfurling petals of a flower—we feel our soul literally begin to expand with joy. We are moving in the direction of wholeness.

Five

What is Real Strength?

"Life is tough, my darling, but so are you."
          ... Stephanie Bennett Henry

Television and movies are full of superheroes with all kinds of challenges. For many of us the words 'strong man' or 'strong woman' conjure up pictures of someone with rippling muscles, or the classic Wonder Woman or Superman with their amazing feats of physical strength. However, there are many kinds of strength. The super heroes themselves say real strength is more than muscles and the ability to pull helicopters from the sky; true strength exhibits integrity, compassion, persistence, commitment and other positive qualities. These reside in the soul and the spirit. The essential, most important kind of strength is about character.

The word 'power' is also often associated with Superheroes, and while strength and power are related, they are not the same. The dictionary defines power as "the capacity or ability to direct or influence the behavior of others or the course of events." There is power that weakens and destroys, and power that strengthens and builds up. The difference is intention.

In the *Star Wars* movies 'the force' is the perfect example of the use and misuse of power. The Emperor, his Empire and Darth Vader are powerful forces for evil. Luke Skywalker, Princess Leia, and (eventually) Han Solo, with the Rebel Forces, use their strength, intelligence and determination as a force for good that ultimately triumphs. We love *The Lord of the Rings* for the same reason: two opposing sides battle for supremacy, one representing good and the other evil.

In many books and movies the lines of dark and light, good and evil, are clearly drawn. Real life, however, is more ambiguous; sometimes it can be difficult to tell the difference between what is good and what is not. Loud voices claim that the whole question of right and wrong is irrelevant anyway, that we should simply do what we feel like doing at the moment. However, there are always consequences to our choices, and when we choose unwisely we run the real risk of reaping a bitter harvest.

In this book we focus on the kind of strength and power that increases light (defined as truth, love, knowledge and understanding) and peace of mind and contributes to individuals and human good in a positive way. Although it is not always immediately apparent, this is the path that brings real and lasting happiness. The battle between the forces of dark and light, good and evil, is always ongoing, both on a large and on a personal scale. When we are truly attuned, when we really listen, our heart and soul does know the difference.

Let's get reacquainted with some folks whose names you are familiar with: **Christopher Reeve**, most famous as Superman in the movies, demonstrated genuine strength in real life after his horse balked at a jump and threw him forward over a wall, leaving him a quadriplegic. After the accident he could move nothing below his chin and was dependent upon others for his every need, breathing only with a medical ventilator that moved air in and out of his lungs. Because of his fame as Superman most of us know his story; the catastrophic fall and subsequent suffering was public in the broadest sense. As a result of that tragedy and in spite of it, using all the resources he could gather including the power of his fame, Reeve, with his wife Dana created the Reeve Foundation that has raised millions of dollars for research toward improving quality of life for those whose lives have been shattered by spinal cord injury. From their own suffering they gained purpose to make a positive difference for good.

Heroes and warriors come in all shapes and sizes. **Mahatma Gandhi** was by appearance, an unlikely one. Yet this small, slender, unassuming attorney, by his character, convictions, leadership and insistence on non-violent solutions literally brought England to its knees, freeing India from the oppressive rule of one of the great world powers of the time. "Strength does not come from physical capacity," Ghandi said, "It comes from an indomitable will . . . You must be the change you wish to see in the world." He demonstrated this with a lifetime of hard work against bitter opposition, arrests and years in jail, and total commitment to what he knew was right. With his wife Kasturba, who was also a political activist, at his side, Gandhi remains one of the most influential men in history, the positive change that rippled out to millions of people, giving hope and inspiration worldwide.

Women are also warriors. Not necessarily in the shoot -'em-up military style, although that is possible, but more frequently by becoming very clear about what is important and right and then doing what is honorable to support that, no matter the obstacles. In most cultures world-wide women are contributing beyond the home and filling additional essential roles in every aspect of society. The recent #MeToo movement empowered women to speak up in cases of sexual abuse, harassment, and discrimination. Black Lives Matter brought racial discrimination to the forefront, and other minorities are also making their voices heard. Human and sex trafficking is being exposed and prosecuted with more vigor than in the past. Hopefully awareness of wrongs is being raised in a way that will benefit people of all different colors, genders and situations. We have much more to accomplish, but because dedicated women and men work hard to make it happen, slowly progress in human rights is being made.

A young woman in Pakistan, **Malala Yousafzai**, became famous worldwide in 2012 when she was shot and critically wounded by the Taliban because she insisted on attending school. She was fifteen years old. During her childhood, as the repressive Taliban rose to power she was an outspoken advocate for the education of girls in her country, giving speeches and blogging anonymously for the BBC. Her stance, supported by her educator father and her mother, defied long standing tradition, and she was well known in Pakistan. Men forced their way onto the bus she was riding home from school and she was shot in the head. Two other girls were wounded.

Malala survived the deadly attack, recovered after several surgeries, and continued her advocacy for women's rights to education. The year following the attack she was asked to address the United Nations. It was her 16th birthday. In 2014 she was awarded the Nobel Peace Prize, the youngest person to ever receive this prestigious award, in her low-key way exhibiting tremendous strength of character, purpose, and courage. The Taliban still considers her a target, yet she continues to advocate for a woman's right to education in those parts of the world where that is often denied.

Florence Nightingale was born into the aristocracy in England in the 1800's. Her sole job was to marry well. Instead, shy young Florence insisted that she follow what she felt was her calling, to be a nurse. Such a course met with shocked disapproval from her family and society; respectable upper class women did not work, and absolutely not in that way—a nurse was considered barely better than a prostitute. Nevertheless she persisted, and found an ally in a respected doctor who supported her efforts. Florence continued to learn nursing care and began to quietly gather and train other women. England was at war, and in an uproar about the neglect of their ill and injured soldiers abroad. When she was in her thirties the Secretary of War asked Florence to organize a corps of nurses to tend to the sick and fallen soldiers 2,000 miles from home. She quickly assembled a team of almost three dozen nurses and a few days later sailed with them to the Crimea. Although they had been warned of the horrid conditions there, nothing could have prepared Nightingale and her nurses for what they saw when they arrived in Constantinople.

The hospital, Scutari, and the water it depended on sat in the middle of what was essentially a large cesspool. Flea and lice infested patients lay helpless in filth while rodents scurried about. There were few medical supplies, bedding, linens or towels. Soap, bandages and water were scarce and the number of patients kept steadily increasing. Soldiers were dying from infection and contagious diseases like typhoid and cholera as much as from the injuries incurred in battle.

Florence went to work 20 hours at a time, leading her helpers in caring for the ill and wounded in more than four miles of closely set beds. The reality must have been beyond overwhelming. Yet by her knowledge, steady persistence and compassion she vastly improved conditions at Scutari and saved many lives. She was a symbol of desperately needed help as she moved about day and night to relieve suffering. The soldiers called her "The Lady with the Lamp." She kept careful records, and returning to England, she used statistics to demonstrate needs, procedures and results to leaders and the medical community. Her conclusions were irrefutable, and this quiet, determined young woman revolutionized the care of the ill and wounded. Florence Nightingale is acknowledged worldwide as "The Mother of Nursing."

Much earlier in England **William Tyndale** was a priest who insisted on translating the Holy Bible from Latin into English, believing that the common people also had a right to read scripture. He did so against the powerful Church of Rome's policy. Because his life was at risk he was forced into hiding abroad, moving from place to place as he labored at the translation. He accomplished his task, and was captured, imprisoned, and in 1536 he was strangled and burned at the stake. But his work could not be undone, and the truths of the Holy Bible were now inalterably in the hands of the people.

Talk of heroes must include **Abraham Lincoln**. Now admired worldwide, the story of his childhood is well known: he was born in a log cabin to poor parents on the rough American frontier and grew up doing manual labor, learning how to work hard. When he discovered books his world opened up. He went from splitting logs for a living to the study and practice of law. He said this about the vocation: "Resolve to be honest at all events; and if in your own judgment you cannot be an honest lawyer, resolve to be honest without being a lawyer." He lived as he spoke and earned the nickname, "Honest Abe."

He fell in love with a young woman who died shortly before they were to be married. After some years he married Mary Todd and fathered four sons, only one of whom lived to adulthood. All his adult life Lincoln suffered from bouts of what he called "melancholy," which today would be diagnosed as clinical depression. He failed repeatedly in business and politics, yet he never gave up. At the age of 52 he was elected President of the United States of America.

The country was in crisis and shuddered apart when the South fired on Fort Sumter. Dismissed with disdain as a 'backwoods country lawyer' by sophisticated Washington D. C., this tall, lanky man with his folksy ways proved to be a wise, able leader during what threatened to be the death throes of a nation. The White House years were filled with heartache: he and his wife grieved the death of their beloved 11-year-old son, while Lincoln bore the heavy burden of leading a country at war with itself that took the lives of at least 620,000 Americans.

Against extreme opposition Lincoln created and put in place the Emancipation Proclamation that freed the slaves, thus dramatically beginning our country's journey toward true equality. He said, "Whenever I hear someone arguing for slavery, I feel a strong impulse to see it tried on him personally," and, "Be sure you put your feet in the right place, then stand firm." That is exactly what he did. When asked how he dealt with his enemies, he said, "I turn them into friends." Quietly, couragously, Lincoln preserved the United States of America and abolished slavery, and for it he was assassinated. At his death a powerful former enemy who had become a staunch supporter, said, "Truly, this was a man for the ages." The world is profoundly better because of this strong, humble, great man.

Although slavery was outlawed on January 1, 1863, racial segregation continued, especially in the southern United States. In the 1960's **Martin Luther King Jr.** responded by speaking out powerfully to advocate civil rights for all Americans, regardless of race or color. While he had supporters of every race, he also had enemies. His "I Have a Dream" speech before 25,000 people in Washington D. C. galvanized the country. Although he repeatedly advocated peaceful solutions, tensions were high and the situation volatile. In 1964 King was awarded the international Nobel Peace Prize. Four years later, despite his stance of non-violence, he too was assassinated for his courageous views and leadership.

Most likely we will not be burned at the stake or shot for a cause we believe in, but it is good to be reminded of privileges we often take for granted, won by the sacrifice of strong people fully committed to doing what they felt was right. They met their circumstances in extraordinary ways, and we are their beneficiaries.

Even heros, however, have their detractors—we have a sad tendency to expect our role models to be perfect, and no human being is without flaws. The heros profiled above were and are real people, of course they were not or are not perfect. This should not be a surprise. We cannot possibly know all the situations and variables any individual is dealing with, or judge why people do what they do by our own perspective and understanding. We can however, appreciate the strength and good we see in others, and learn from it.

When we study the lives of men and women who inspire and uplift we see that their roads were not easy; adversity played a large part in shaping them into who they became. Winston Churchill, the strong-willed Prime Minister of England during the dark days of World War II, said, "Kites rise highest against the wind—not with it." So it is for the world-changers, and so it is for us. Despite difficulties, and there will be difficulties, whether the scope of our influence be large or small, we have the potential, the opportunity, and the responsibility to change our own worlds for the better.

Social scientists have identified a characteristic that strong, successful people invariably have. It is resilience. It is that quality that enables a rubber ball to bounce back up when it has been thrown to the floor. In fact, it is the force of the throw that determines how high the ball will bounce. Likewise, even though a personal blow may be powerful and briefly over-whelming, resilient people have the ability to recover, and even though they may be staggering, get their feet beneath them again and find the strength to continue on. Studies have shown that more than any other, it is this quality that makes the difference in whether humans thrive or not as they deal with the difficult challenges that come into all lives.

The lack of resilience can play out in tragic ways. A friend recently told of a family he knew that lost a child to death. The mother never recovered and a second young child went without the love and attention she desperately needed and did not receive after the death of her older sibling. At an informal study group I attended a few years ago, for our first meeting we each took a couple of minutes to tell a little about ourselves. The major part of one middle-aged woman's introduction to this group of mostly strangers was, "I was raped when I was sixteen." Sexual abuse is traumatizing, and especially so before the age of eighteen. I am certain this was a horrific, scarring experience. Yet how sad that this intelligent, warm-hearted woman continues to define herself foremost in this way more than forty years later. I wish there had been someone to give the support and assistance that could have helped her to recover.

I do not mean to downplay the pain of trauma and loss. I know them. But recovery is possible. The scars may never completely disappear, but they can heal. Now, with more awareness of the damage caused by such experiences, significant help is available to do so. It is important because when our wounds become the essence of how we define ourselves they can cripple us, and the loss of our lives as fully functioning human beings may become an ongoing tragedy. Clearly, resilience matters a great deal.

So how do we get this important quality, resilience? Is it something we are born with, like blonde hair or brown eyes? Do we learn or not learn it from our families? Perhaps some of both. It is a quality we are born with—if our bodies were healthy, didn't we all persist in learning to walk, despite failing many times? Other failures and challenges will continue to come as we move through our lives. We can overcome them also. For some, the instinct for quick recovery comes naturally. Others may have never learned good coping skills, or been dealt so many blows that they have lost hope that things can change for the better. While there is much we can do ourselves, we may need professional help. The important thing is that we find a way to develop and incorporate resilience into our lives.

Often, when the need is extreme we reach down into our deepest resources and somehow find the strength to carry on. When the storm clouds are heavy, thick and dark and the way seems blocked, these are the times you learn that you are stronger than you knew, and smarter. Perhaps a different approach is needed, or an altered perspective. By its very nature resilience includes flexibility, and usually patience, and faith that although things may not go exactly the way we want, they will happen in the way they should when the time is right. Resilience says, "Yes, I may be battered, but I am not beaten. I can get through this. I am strong. I can do what is required."

Being resilient does not mean we pretend we weren't hurt, it means we find a way to recover.

Real strength wears many faces. My friend Judy was first raped by a Catholic priest when she was barely 10 years old. It continued into her 12th year. He told her of course, that this must be a secret. Her family trusted this man completely and she had been taught to look to him as the one who had the answers. Finally she thought, "This cannot be right, it *can't* be." She spoke to someone about what had been happening, and help was given. Now Judy is in a healthy marriage and has channeled her anger and sorrow about the destruction of her childhood into activism to protect children. She is a public speaker to schools and community groups and has been a major force in educating lawmakers to enact protective legislation in her state and nationally. Judy is resilient, and a powerful force for good.

Two more of my most admired strong, resilient people are Curtis and Diana.

Diana was a warm, vivacious, beautiful brunette, wife of a busy yet supportive husband and the mother of two adored daughters. When she was a teenager, Diana was in an auto accident that sent her through the window and rammed her head against a mountain. It damaged her spine, and from that time on she lived in severe pain most of the time. Operation after operation made little difference, and so she put on a happy face and did the best she could. Unless you knew her well, you were not aware of what she suffered.

We had just moved to Tucson, Arizona, and knew no one there. Eight months after we arrived I became seriously ill and was bedridden most of the time. I told the story in an earlier chapter: within the next year my husband was fired from his job, soon we lost our beautiful home, and serious long-time problems in our marriage ended in divorce. It was real crisis, and I was talking to no one about any of it.

Diana made it a point to befriend me. I did not realize then how desperately I needed a friend, but I knew how much I enjoyed Diana. With her, for the first time, it felt safe to open up and talk about my life. As I came to know her I learned that she volunteered at the hospital emergency room and Hospice. Her husband Doug had heavy responsibilities as the layman leader of our congregation and Diana also spent hours helping. I asked once how she did it all. She said, "I feel better when I'm helping others."

She would call to see if I could come over, and if I was able to drive I would. She needed to lie down often because her back hurt, and I needed to lie down because I was sick and aching and too exhausted to stay upright, so we would lie kitty-corner on their huge king-size bed, our heads propped up on pillows at opposite corners, and talk, and laugh and cry. It was healing for both of us.

A few years later life took me out of state and Doug and Diana went to Portugal for two years as leaders of a large church mission. Shortly after they returned I came back to Tucson but was far across the city, and with both our health challenges our interaction was on the phone. Her family called one day to tell me that Diana had died from complications related to surgery. She was 44. At her funeral I learned how many other people she had blessed. More than 2,000 people came to honor her, and many of them felt as I did, that they had lost their best friend. Diana was not world-famous, but she had true strength that was based on faith and loving others, and her bright spirit and genuine caring was life-changing for many people.

Like Diana, Curtis is another who epitomizes strength. Curt was one of those little boys who to all appearances never stopped moving. He had a quick grin, dark hair that went every which way, and blue eyes that sparkled with mischief. He was always either up a tree, teasing his family or earnestly telling them fascinating facts he'd learned from reading the family's set of encyclopedia. He mortified his shy older sister each day walking home from school because he liked to lunge toward the street and make crazy faces at the cars driving by. He caught lizards or chipmunks or any other small wild creature possible, and took good care of them until he released them. During elementary school he caught and trained hawks to ride on his small, leather covered arm.

However, from two years old, breathing was sometimes a challenge for him. When he was three his parents drove more than 400 miles to visit specialists at a renowned children's hospital, where after 2 ½ weeks the problem was diagnosed as asthma. That turned out to be only partially correct. Throughout his childhood there continued sometimes to be wakeful nights and days of inactivity because the effort to breathe demanded all his energy.

After serving two years in England on a church mission while a young man, he came home with a respiratory condition so severe that two-thirds of one lung had to be removed. He attended college, married and raised children, but healthwise, things deteriorated. During his thirties he developed a horrific deep cough that did not go away. Doctors didn't know how to help, and over several years his lung capacity diminished until he needed oxygen 24 hours a day—for 22 years he was tethered day and night to an oxygen tank by a 50 ft. hose. Throughout, his grin and sense of humor remained.

Determined, he worked to support his family as a skilled craftsman in wood, and volunteered many hours with church responsibilities including leadership, and helping neighbors, family and friends. He was in and out of the hospital frequently with pneumonia or related issues and eventually his lung capacity dropped to only13%. He made application to receive a double lung transplant. After eight months he was approved, and in the qualification process was diagnosed as having a rare form of Cystic Fibrosis. Finally, an explanation for the life-long struggle for air.

He underwent a double lung transplant, and while dealing with the quality of life complications that can result from that he can now breathe and be active, and determinedly still maintains a positive outlook on life. And he is still helping others. To my "How are you doing?" question, a cheerful, "Well, I'm not dying as fast as people thought I would!" response is typical—even during the bad times he usually ends up making the questioner laugh. Supporting him through all of this was and is Ruth, his patient, strong, loving wife and companion. She is amazing in her own right. There is no bitterness, and I have never heard either of them whine or complain. Curtis is my brother. Although he would laugh if I told him so, he is one of the strongest men I know.

True strength is all around us—if we knew the stories of many of the people we meet and interact with, we would find we are surrounded by examples of courage and strength. Most often the stories remain unknown except to a few.

In the small book *The Little Prince* by Antoine de Saint-Exupéry, is this quote: "It is only with the heart that one can see rightly; what is essential is invisible to the eye." And so it is. The important strengths that will carry us through our journey are invisible to the eye: courage to make good decisions; respect and love for others and self; commitment to principle as we move toward our goals; faith in the outcome; doing our best and picking ourselves up and going again when we fall; holding onto hope even in the darkest times—and much, much more. All seen and understood by the heart.

We can of course, choose to simply continue as we are wherever we are, dreaming endlessly on a mountaintop, or drifting along with the current wherever it takes us. It is the easier way. But if we desire more, if we want our lives to be better, we need to awaken and initiate the process of change. It will be worth it. There are pressing causes to support and fight for, and willing warriors are always needed. Or, our enemies may be personal and intangible, with names like pride, indecision, selfishness, fear, laziness, arrogance, procrastination, or negativity. These and their brothers weaken us. It takes courage to face and conquer them.

The Superheroes we enjoy watching don't stand idly by. They take positive action against the forces that would stop them. They make things happen. So can we. If we do not make things happen in our lives, who will? Know that when our motivation is true and good, God stands ever ready to help us. With each step forward we become stronger and stronger in ourselves and in Him. Strengthening the good in ourselves and around us, despite the opposition—this is the strength that matters most. This is real strength.

Six

You Have To Want It!

"The starting point of all achievement is desire... Weak desires bring weak results, just as a small amount of fire makes a small amount of heat."

. . . . . Napoleon Hill

How do some people manage to deal so well with their challenges? How can we? There is a powerful symbiosis between our own efforts and that force in the universe that desires our best good. There is an unfolding, growing process that begins with our waking up and realizing that we want things to be different. In this chapter we will explore the activating power of focused desire.

A pivotal awakening happened for me at my son's junior high school. He needed to change a class and I waited in the counselor's office until she returned and could sign the necessary paper. On the counselor's wall in front of me was a poster at least three feet high. It was titled: "*I Have a Right.*" It began:

- I have a right to be treated with respect.
- I have a right to express how I feel and what I think.
- I have a right to have my needs be as important as the needs of others.
- I have a right to be myself.
- I have a right not to be abused by anyone in any way.

More rights followed.

As I read that list, it hit me like the shock of a revelation. I recognized the truth of it—of course, these are basic human rights and everyone should have them. But they did not apply to the way my life was! Clearly, something was wrong and needed to change. (This list of *Personal Rights* is in the Appendix. The United Nations has created its own broader list, *A Universal Declaration of Human Rights* which you can find online.)

We have talked in previous chapters about the faulty programming caused by neglect of emotional and/or physical needs, abuse, trauma and other negative experiences, and the distorted thinking and behavior they produce. Now that we realize that this can and does happen, if we see evidence of it in our lives we must decide if we want something different. If so, we must believe that change is possible and take action. You have within you all that it takes to make that happen. We hope, we plan, and work for the best possible outcome, and sometimes we achieve exactly what we desire. Other times things may not work out exactly the way we planned. And sometimes, to our surprise, all works out even better than we expected.

During the years I was twelve and thirteen I suddenly shot up from comfortably being one of the smaller girls in elementary school, to one of the tall ones in junior high. I was beanpole thin with brown hair and glasses—wondering if I was ever going to have any curves, and self-conscious about all of it. My best friend was Lorraine. We were always together. She had big blue eyes, shining long blonde hair and a generous figure curvy in all the right places. When we entered high school at fourteen, Lorraine was soon dating a senior on the football team. As we walked together in the halls people would call out, "Hi, Lorraine!" I seemed to be invisible, and that, I decided, did not feel good. I wasn't interested in being the center of attention, but I did want people to acknowledge I was there. Lorraine was spending a lot of time with her boyfriend, and I realized I needed to make additional friends if school was going to be fun. So I did.

Lorraine and I were still friends, but I started joining clubs and paying attention to other people also. Understanding how it felt to be invisible, I was friendly to everyone, and quickly learned that there were many friends to be made. At the end of that year Lorraine's family moved out of state. I had adjusted to seeing less of her, and while I missed her, I knew it would be all right. It was.

During my sophomore year I grew out of the gawky, self-conscious phase. I genuinely liked people, and they responded with friendship. By my junior year I had plenty of dates to choose from, had been elected to positions of leadership in the class and clubs, won several awards, was elected to be a student body officer for our senior year, winning state honors and offices also. High school turned out to be very fun indeed.

When I decided I wanted things to be different as a freshman I didn't really understand what I had set in motion, only that I was unhappy and that it was up to me to change things. Feeling insecure and unnoticed, my desire was simply to improve the situation; I did not set out with specific goals to be a leader. However, that was the end result. Sometimes, life surprises us with an unexpected abundance of good.

I hadn't really processed that experience in a larger context until a parakeet forcefully brought the power of focused desire to my attention. It happened when I was just beginning to awaken to the seriousness of the problems in my marriage. I didn't realize it, but I had been very good at avoidance for a long time.

One day in Tucson I was halfway across the city and had a little extra time between appointments. Just for fun, I decided to go into a nearby pet store to look at the animals. Immediately inside the door was a waist-high platform supporting a sturdy, leafless, five-foot tall section of a branched tree,

covered with what seemed like hundreds of colorful, fluttering parakeets. They were all the same, an unusual mix with
white and yellow breasts and vibrant turquoise, blue and green
on the back and wings. I had never seen any like them. They
were not caged, but stayed on the tree, a chirruping, shifting, living kaleidoscope. I gasped and stood motionless in
admiration, and with my whole being I wanted one of those
lovely creatures. After some time my reason asserted itself,
and I said, "Linda, you do not need a parakeet, for goodness
sakes!" After some lingering looks I went about my business
and forgot about them.

Two weeks later I came home from running errands, and
there, walking about on the welcome mat before the front
door, was one of those uniquely-colored parakeets. Delighted,
I said, "Hello, you beautiful thing! Don't go away, I'll be right
back," and edged around and through the door, thinking hard
about what I had to keep it in. It spent a couple of days in
one upside down laundry basket fastened to another one right
side up, until I bought a proper cage with the necessary gear.

A similar incident happened a few months later. A friend
and I had enjoyed visiting a rock shop where I learned about
geodes. They were entrancing, their ugly rough exterior hiding
beautiful crystals inside—if ever there was a splendid example
of "Don't judge a book by its cover" it is a geode. I yearned to
have one. That desire floated to the surface several times, but
I did not intend to do anything about it.

Our Tucson home on its 1/3 acre lot was set well back from the street, surrounded by natural desert with its various spiny, prickly plants, typical of this Sonoran Desert country. One morning I had pulled the trash barrel to the street and was trudging back to the house through the cactus and mesquite, rabbitbrush and ocotillo, and there, lying at my feet, was a perfect geode as big around as the palm of my hand. In our yard!

I have the geode still—I have not had it sawn in half to see what crystallized splendor hides inside; I prefer it as it is, holding mystery. And that sweet little bird lived with our family for thirteen years. I knew the arrival of both the parakeet and the geode so close together held profound meaning of some sort; it has taken years for me to gain understanding. While there may be yet more to realize from the parakeet and the geode both showing up literally at my feet, thus far I have learned:

- That there is real power in focused desire.
- That I was permitted to want something and receive it.
- That I mattered to God. The fact that He was paying attention was inescapable; He was the only one who could have known I wanted a parakeet and a geode, and only He could have given them to me. He noticed, and He cared about me in a tender, personal way. This was a life-altering shift of perception.
- God knew hard times were immediately ahead for me, and that it was important I go through them for my

growth. He gave me these sweet gifts that I could see, touch, hold and be comforted, remembering how they came to me.

- That God sometimes uses symbols. The cheerful, pretty little bird that brightened my days was a living reminder that beauty is God's signature and it is all around us. The geode was a reminder that appearances can be deceiving. Who would imagine that the rough, ugly exterior could hold such wonders inside? Unpleasant things, or experiences, can have unexpected value.

These are lessons I want to remember.

Some would call these experiences 'Manifesting Desire,' which seems accurate but not quite adequate. Some say that whatever we really want will inevitably come to us. I don't believe this is always so. Certainly there have been times in my life when I wanted something very much that did not happen, and plenty of things that happened that I absolutely did not want. Probably you have experienced the same.

I believe that while we can greatly impact what comes into our lives, there are times when God has something different in mind for us. When that is the case we can count on the fact that there are important reasons for it, even though we may not see them at the time. And my experience says that if we are patient and flexible, that alternative will in the long run be the best possible scenario. What we do always have control over is the way we respond to what life brings to us.

In this too, desire plays a role. When we are determined that somehow even the storm clouds will eventually turn out to have a silver lining, we tremendously improve our chances of a positive outcome.

There is no question that focused, even burning desire is an essential element in real accomplishment of any kind. Whether learning to play the piano to become a concert pianist, climbing Mount Everest, building our own home or buying one, finding a job that fits our specific skills and needs—whatever it may be, first we have to want it. Really want it. The more focused and specific we can be, the more clearly those desires can be brought into reality. Most often that includes doing the necessary work to bring it about; the fulfilling may come into being so slowly we barely recognize it is happening. And sometimes, unexpectedly and wonderfully, the Universe gifts us in ways that manifest as quickly and simply as a parakeet and a geode.

A further aspect of this quality of focused desire has been called 'intention.' Self Improvement guru Wayne Dyer speaks of the concept in his several excellent books and videos, specifically in *The Power of Intention*. He contends that passion, not the romantic kind, but a vigorous enthusiasm difficult to explain or define but that you feel deep within, is essential to fulfilling our dreams. The Greek word for enthusiasm is 'entheos,' which means "God is in us." This may be the best definition of all.

Goethe, the German philosopher, author and statesman, expands further with "commitment." He clarifies with the following powerful statement: "Until one is committed, there is hesitancy . . . ineffectiveness. The moment one definitely commits oneself, then Providence moves too. All sorts of things occur to help one that would never otherwise have occurred. A whole stream of events in one's favor come his way. Boldness has genius, power and magic in it. Whatever you can do or dream you can. . . . begin it now!"

Many thinking people through the ages have come to the same conclusion. In the ancient scriptures called the Old Testament of the Holy Bible, Proverb 23 says, "As a man thinketh in his heart . . . so is he." When we open our eyes and look around us it is an evident truth—we can see it in the lives of others and in our own lives. What we focus our thoughts and energy on grows and gains power in our life. By focusing on and desiring more strength and abundance and believing it is coming, we draw it to us and it increases. The opposite is also true. Habitual negative thinking can literally steal our lives away from us. If either by patterning, disposition or habit we tend to find ourselves usually focusing on the negative, it will become larger and larger in our lives.

Everyone is discouraged and depressed at times; life is made up of both sunshine and shadow for all of us. There are times when life just stinks, and pretending otherwise is neither helpful nor productive. Remember that it will pass. Hard times will pass. It can help to remind ourselves. Long-term ongoing depression however, is a different matter that requires special attention; counseling and medication are appropriate and perhaps necessary. But for the ups and downs that assail everyone at times, simply being aware of our thoughts and feelings and knowing they are temporary can help us begin to find our way to positivity.

So, is the gas tank really half full or half empty? It is both. But numerous scientific studies have shown that focusing on the negative literally, measurably drains energy from us, while focusing on the positive creates energy. We can feel the difference. We certainly are not in control of everything, but we have much, much more control then we often realize. My grandfather used to say, "It takes no special ability to stand by and criticize—any idiot can do it." No one likes to be around a perpetually gloomy Gus or Gertie, and it isn't any fun for Gus or Gertie either! We are capable of so much more. Yes, painful things do happen. And acknowledging that we are hurting, that we feel what we feel, is important. Yet making a conscious choice about our further response determines the tone of our life.

Gratitude is a powerful healer. We can help ourselves by choosing to be positive and grateful for blessings, even for such basics as being able to walk, or talk, or see. Not everyone can. The day I drove to downtown Tucson to file bankruptcy I was waiting at a stoplight in a poor neighborhood, discouraged right down to the bottom of the barrel. I heard music, and rolling toward me on the sidewalk were two young teenagers. They were both on skateboards, one holding a boombox on his shoulder. The other propelled himself along at ground level with his hands, because he had no legs. They were laughing and singing and having a grand good time. I sat stunned for a moment as they whizzed by, and my attitude did an immediate, dramatic shift. Yes, things were bad for me, but I had much to be grateful for.

We do not have to be the passive victim of the downward spiral negativity precipitates. If you wake up feeling particularly grumpy you can decide this is not how you want to start the day and change it—begin counting blessings and fill your mind with positive thoughts and energy. It may not solve all the problems, but it will certainly help you feel better! If feeling grateful is not your accustomed mindset, start paying attention and develop it. Gratitude is a dynamic force: use it to improve your life.

Remember that just as the wake of a boat indicates where the boat has gone but does not determine where it is going, your past is behind you. It does not, need not, determine your future. You are driving the boat. You are in charge, and you choose what happens next.

It has been said many times and it remains true: "The world steps aside for the man or woman who knows where they are going." That person can be you. Utilizing the power of focused desire and intention can bring into being what you dream of.

As we follow the Sleeping Maiden on her way, we see that she awoke, arose, determined where she wanted to go, and acted. She was bound by her past no longer. You have awakened. Shake off the chains that previously bound you, leave them where they lie and walk away. Desire and commitment activate your powerful spirit, mind, and body. With intention, a clear, focused mind, a healing and compassionate heart and eyes that see limitless possibilities, you stride with compelling determination into a brighter future.

Seven

Be Real And Heal

"There are some people who live in a dream world, and there are some who face reality; and then there are those who turn one into the other . . ."

..... Douglas H. Everett

Turning our dreams into reality requires 'getting real.' And facing reality can sometimes be very hard indeed. We human beings are good at avoidance, conscious and unconscious. There are always reasons: the pain we do not want to feel may come from something we did or did not do that caused harm in some way, and remembering is so painful that we bury it deep down and refuse to look at it. It could come from the hurtful actions of another person, and refusing to really 'see' or talk or think about it keeps the pain at bay so we can avoid dealing with it. The reality could be something terrible that we were powerless to prevent, the trauma so severe that our mind places the experience into our unconscious to protect our ability to function.

Consciously or unconsciously burying hurtful memories can work temporarily. Yet the reality affects us, even when we are not aware. Avoiding pain, physical, mental or emotional, is a natural human response, and at times doing so protects us. However, when past trauma or injury is unresolved, the memories do remain—our spirit, our brain, our very cells remember, and eventually the accompanying emotion will surface in some form or another and demand that we deal with it. To heal, we must find a way to face what is.

New research shows that the consequences of avoidance can be serious. Candace Pert, former Chief of the Section on Brain Biochemistry of the Clinical Neuroscience Branch at the National Institute of Mental Health, studies health influences at the neurochemical level. She noted recently that "Repressing emotions can be causative of disease. Failure to find effective ways to express negative emotions causes you to 'stew in your own toxic juices." Paraphrasing and simplifying information from the website www.cellularmemory. org where she is quoted, she explains that emotions produce chemicals which regulate how our bodies function. Negative emotions produce harmful chemicals that cause damage to body systems. Suppressed emotion is not the cause of all disease, but it is a significant contributor. This is serious business. Clearly, it is important to find healthy, healing ways to deal with the negative emotions of our lives.

I have come to believe that the chronic illness that has so impacted my life developed partially from the very reason Dr. Pert speaks of—my inability to recognize and acknowledge emotional pain and severe stress over an extended period of time. For self-preservation from early childhood I had learned not to acknowledge or express feelings; I did not realize I was doing so or that the way I was functioning was unhealthy. But our bodies, our hearts and minds are inextricably linked, and I believe that finally my body could not handle the stress any longer. I am doing all I can to heal, and have finally accepted that the damage is not something I can repair by willing it to be different. Accepting what is lays the groundwork for finding adaptations that are helpful and hopeful. As we all do, I deal with my reality in the best way I can.

Usually people are doing the best they can. Every person's story is their own, and seldom do we know all the details. While it is important to make judgements about what we make part of our own lives, we are rarely in a position to make judgements about others.

Suffering forced me to really look at some truths in my life. It's hard to know which came first—the physical pain of the illness or the emotionally painful awakening, but they are connected. Together it was a little like being whacked alongside the head with a 2x4. In slow motion. But—both carried gifts within them that opened the way for healing.

At one point during my journey a counselor showed me a small figurine of a brightly smiling woman whose body from the waist down disappeared into the gaping maw of a huge shark. "This typifies you, Linda, more than any client I have worked with." That was alarming. "Hm," I said. This was important information—a strong message that for self-protection, changes in my automatic responses would be wise. With thought I realized that, yes, that 'keep smiling no matter what' approach was true of me, and in some situations, it did contribute to a serious problem. On the other hand, a naturally sunny disposition and positive outlook have been a true advantage at times, helping me through extremely difficult situations and sometimes protecting me.

What is essential, I learned, is balance. Every characteristic, every quality, is a double-edged sword cutting two directions. Both positive and negative taken to excess, can become a liability.

Ignoring painful realities is not uncommon—psychologists sometimes call it 'the elephant in the room.' The huge, room-filling entity is there causing problems, but either consciously or unconsciously one carries on as if it were not. Inevitably, at some point there is a consequence.

Being human, we all have our quirks and blind spots, we can't help it—we are formed by and function out of our physiology, our experiences, and our perceptions. When we find ourselves dealing with the same difficult issues again and again however, it is a signal to pay attention; there is probably some-thing important we need to learn. Truths we are unwilling to see may show up as difficult relationships with family, friends or co-workers, poor health, a nagging sense of something 'not right,' or in a myriad of other ways. The problem may be something within ourselves, or someone else, or in the situa-tion. An essential first step to improvement is what some call 'surrender to what is.' The past happened, we can't change it. Whatever is, is. Only in being willing to truthfully acknowl-edge what may have happened or is currently happening can we figure out how to best deal with it and find peace of mind. This is a process that requires attention, honesty, commitment, compassion for ourselves and for others, patience, and cour-age. It is worth it.

"One might notice," says M. Catherine Thomas in *Light In the Wilderness*, "that healing comes from changing oneself rather than another person."

An intelligent, capable friend of mine went through three jobs over a period of several years. In each she had a boss who bullied and mistreated her and eventually she quit. After the third, the light dawned and she began to realize that she was allowing herself to be treated badly. She knew that she deserved respect and decided she would accept nothing less. With that change in her attitude, she went into interviews with a different mindset. Soon came a job where she was treated well and appreciated.

Because human experiences and needs vary so widely, there is a tremendous body of literature about healing—physical, mental, emotional and spiritual (which are all interrelated), and a multitude of approaches. There is Western medicine, Eastern medicine, conventional and traditional and non-traditional, naturopathic, integrative, spiritual, psychotherapy, and more, each with their own multiple subheadings. Enthusiastic advocates sometimes are absolutely certain that their way is the best possible way to achieve a certain outcome, and perhaps for them it is. It might be equally helpful to you, or it might not. No one can really tell you what will best meet your needs except you yourself, which means each of us must take an active role in this process. As you learn to open your mind and listen to your heart, certain information will resonate with you in a positive way. You will feel that this is something you need to investigate further.

Suffering and unhappiness wear many faces, and an essential factor in genuine healing is the necessity of dealing with our reality. We can avoid it, but there is a price.

Here is Melanie's story:

"Jeff and I had been married for sixteen years before I could deal with what was happening in our marriage. There were problems I thought were serious, but when I brought them up he stonewalled me and refused to talk about anything. Our four kids seemed to be doing pretty well and everyone else thought we were

doing great, so I buried my thoughts and feelings and pretended everything was fine.

Eventually, evidence surfaced that he was being unfaithful, and it had been happening for years. It became obvious that he had lied to me about that and other related things. When I confronted him he denied everything at first, but the evidence was absolutely clear. He would not accept responsibility for his behavior and I could not continue living as we had been. When he realized I really was filing for divorce, things started to change. He didn't want to lose his family, and I finally decided to stay together while we began working with a counselor.

Both of us have had to face some difficult truths. It has been extremely hard for me to trust him again. But we are learning how to be more honest with each other and ourselves, and the counselor is teaching us new ways to communicate. We are both committed to making the marriage work. There are still ups and downs of course, but things between us are better now than they have ever been, and I think it will keep getting better."

It usually is easier to try to ignore something, at least temporarily—we can keep limping along, pretending everything is A-OK. To really fix a problem however, it must be clearly defined, and this requires being willing to look at what may be hard to face. While getting to that point is usually under our control, sometimes, for good reasons, it is not.

The following experience may seem extreme, but variations of it apply to a surprising number of people. It demonstrates another aspect of how hidden trauma can severely impact lives.

Here is Suzanne's story: *"There are three children in my family, myself and my much younger brothers. My brothers seemed to get along fine with my father, but he was physically and emotionally cruel to me from as early as I can remember. He was really mean to me, yelling and smacking me a lot. I was always afraid when I was around him; I couldn't seem to do anything that didn't make him mad.*

When I was in my thirties I began having brief moments of intense negative feelings accompanied by a memory of being very small and being held so tightly I couldn't move, by a strong grownup forcing me to do something unpleasant. They happened a number of times for several years. I was puzzled by them, but they stopped and I forgot about them. (I had not heard the term then, now I know these are called 'flashbacks.') Then several years later I suddenly had a clear memory of a specific male adult family member coming into my room and sexually abusing me when I was a toddler. With the memory came an overwhelming, horrible feeling of fear, outrage and helplessness. I don't know how many times the sexual abuse happened, but the memory was not the first time. I understood then what the flashbacks had been about.

I thought I could be okay and forget about it, but after two weeks of being barely able to function because I was usually in tears, I realized I needed some professional help. I met with a counselor who helped me work through the hurt and anger that surfaced, and to see how all of the abuse has impacted my life, even though I wasn't aware of the sexual part of it for so long. Many years later I am still dealing with its effects.

Although I would like to marry, on a deep level I don't get 'how' to have a healthy close relationship with a man. I haven't made good choices, even though I want to. There are other issues also, including PTSD (Post Traumatic Stress Syndrome). Years of counseling have helped, and I am healing. The anxiety I lived with all the time and wasn't even aware of has gone way down. I am still not where I want to be, but I am calmer and stronger and emotionally healthier than I have ever been."

Such experiences and worse, do happen, and sometimes serious damage has been done. If we knew the stories of the people around us we might be horrified at what some have endured. Likewise, we can be deeply impressed, even amazed, at what some have managed to rise above and overcome.

Problems hiding an underlying truth that we are blind to could be such concerns as: "My boss is a jerk who demeans me and takes credit for my ideas. I am sick of it." Or, "My daughter is no longer the sweet girl she was a year ago. She has drastically changed and she won't talk to me. How can I find out what is going on with her?" Or, "Our business is in a neighborhood that is going down fast. We keep pouring money into it, but we are close to bankruptcy. What are we going to do?" Or, "Bob/Sue/Gina/Trevor or (you insert a name) and I have been dating for five years and he/she waffles every time I talk about commitment. Is this ever going to change?" Or, "Every time a relationship begins getting serious, I find a way to sabotage it. What is going on?"

Help is available from different sources. An insightful book with a novel approach by Charles Whitfield, M.D. and psychoanalyst, is titled *Healing the Child Within.* He suggests that few of us received fully adequate parenting, usually because our parents did not know a better way, and that this affects us to varying degrees. He teaches how to differentiate between our inner (wise) Adult Voice and the voice of our Wounded Inner Child. We can facilitate healing by acknowledging these unrecognized early wounds. We can, as a Wise Adult, say words that were needed but not given to our Inner Child, such as:

- "You were an innocent child. You did not deserve to be hurt/mistreated/neglected/abused."
- "You deserve love. You are loveable." Say it into the mirror and mean it!
- "It is alright to feel hurt, or sad, or afraid, or angry . . . We'll find a way through this. It's going to be okay."
- "I am sorry I didn't listen to you before. I didn't know how, but now I do."
- I forgive you for mistakes. You are human and imperfect like everyone else."
- "You did the best you could, and you are amazing!

- Look how far you've come and how well you've done!"
- Thank you for never giving up even though it was so hard. Thank you for being so strong, and protecting me the best way you knew."

In doing this we address the unmet needs of that wounded Inner Child who may never have been given loving support or reassurance. We can appreciate what the child endured, and nurture and re-parent him or her as a wise, caring adult. This can be a foundation for further work.

There are plenty of adults walking around, who under stress, behave like a three-year-old. We can learn to recognize emotional immaturity in others and in ourselves, and know that healing is needed. Self-knowledge is the prelude to progress. We cannot fix others, and excusing abusive or toxic behaviour from any source helps no one. We have the right and responsibility to protect ourselves and those we are appropriately responsible for. Our growth into healthier, happier, more whole adults is a duty and privilege we can relegate to no one but ourselves.

If we continue to rationalize, pull the covers over our head or put blinders on our eyes and keep smiling as if all is just dandy, at some point the painful consequences of inaction will probably insist that we face reality and do something different. Just like an untended physical injury, the traumatised part can fester until the whole organism is harmed. Emotional damage is just as real as physical injury, and just as important.

Some years ago a small, exotic-looking plant showed up in my flower bed. I had never seen one like it, and curious, I decided to let it grow and see what it became. I was busy and paid little attention to it for a while, and the next time I really looked it had grown into a sturdy monster almost four feet high. It was producing nothing at all and using great amounts of the resources my garden needed. Pulling on it with all my strength didn't budge it from the ground. The stalk was so thick I had to use a hatchet to cut it down, and then laboriously dig out the deep root with a shovel. The analogy to our lives is unavoidable: the sooner we identify and pull out the weeds, so to speak, the easier it will be.

Kylie is a good example of someone who has made the decision to make changes and is following through. She says: *"I made some serious mistakes when I was younger. I started smoking early, and then got into heavy partying with drinking and drugs. I got pregnant and had an abortion. Twice. My relationship with my parents was never good and it kept getting worse. Finally they didn't want anything to do with me. I didn't care.*

It took being in jail and three and a half years in prison before I began to admit that I had made a mess of my life. The hardest part was to believe that I really could change and my life could be different—I was so used to seeing myself as a total mess-up. But I did want to change, and once I decided, I found that there were people and programs to help. After getting out of prison one of the hardest things was staying away from the former 'friends' and situations that sucked me back into old patterns. But with support, I'm doing it.

I've been clean, off drugs and alcohol for more than a year. I have a real job now. I am trying to build a better relationship with my parents; I don't know how that is going to go —they don't trust me yet, and I can understand why. If that doesn't work out it will hurt, but I will be okay. I'm learning, and I'm getting stronger. It's been a long, hard road, but things really are getting better."

The first thing Kylie had to do was to honestly, clearly see her reality. Instead of blaming everything and everyone else, she took responsibility for her past, present and future. She wanted a better life, she realized she needed help, and got it. She knew that the road was not going to be easy, yet she committed and persisted and is making truly impressive progress. She recognizes that how her parents and the other people in her life react is up to them; she has no control over their behavior. She is working hard on her challenges and building the life she wants. As she continues along that path her sense of self-worth will grow and she will become stronger and more and more capable. As you make the changes you desire in your life, so will you.

A wise man said, "Pray as if everything depends on God; work as if everything depends upon you." Only when we realistically, honestly acknowledge the truths of our lives, the dark and the light, the sad and glad, and take responsibility for what is within our power to change, can we make genuine progress. Only then can we truly heal. Even though it may go slowly and feel overwhelming at times, do not give up. Your path is uniquely yours. We are all different with individual experiences and varying needs. And we all have it within ourselves to recognize our own reality and make whatever changes we desire.

Recognizing and correcting the deep inroads of habitual negative thinking, feelings and behavior that exert such power over our lives is life-changing, and it is a lifelong commitment. Once on the path, step by step we will see and feel the improvements, and if we choose to make it so, the results will be tremendously satisfying and truly marvelous. If we want things to be better, we can choose to wake up, rise up, and take action.

Remember, there is a power in the universe that wants your success and your happiness. When something good unexpectedly occurs, some call it serendipity. I believe it is much more personal than that. God is paying attention, and you will receive aid and gifts along your way, as I have—a parakeet, or a geode, or a free glass tabletop exactly the right size when I was too poor to buy one for the beautiful coffee table base my brother had made for me. You'll happen upon the 'too expensive' jacket you've been wanting at 75% off just when you need it, or receive a friendly card or text or plate of cookies when you feel no one in the world cares one bit about you. Out of the blue you'll have a sudden flash of inspiration that solves a problem you've despaired of solving—blessings will come to you, specifically to meet your needs.

When the universe unexpectedly presents us with our desires as it sometimes does, I believe it is to let us know that we are noticed and loved by One much stronger, wiser and greater than we are. God is saying to us, "You matter. You are so important to me that I am listening to the very desires of your heart. Here is a gift just for you." This is precious, priceless validation, especially when we feel discouraged, hurt, or forgotten. To recognize these for what they are, we must be paying attention. To help remember, write them down. They can buoy you up through the rough patches.

God knows our road is not easy. And just as a butterfly will not develop properly if we unwrap its cocoon, or a baby chick will be weakened by our breaking its eggshell, He knows our journey is something we must do ourselves. He is always there, helping appropriately, and expressing His love to us in ways we often do not recognize.

A magnificent gift to all is the wonder of nature. From the amazing potential contained within a seed to the elegant marvel of DNA, from lush blooms of cactus in the desert to ocean waves crashing onto jagged cliffs and galaxies wheeling through star-studded space, the interconnected complexity and overarching simplicity of nature powerfully testifies of a supreme organizing Intelligence. With what perfection are both function and aesthetics addressed in the geometry of fractals and the sweeping curves of the Fibonacci sequence—logic and beauty both fulfilled in the marvelous structures of life and earth and sky. When we pay attention to the natural world around us, when we become still and absorb its wonder and peace, there is a pure, profound truth at its core that speaks to our soul. Nature supports our very being, and promotes both tangible and intangible healing.

God's gifts are meant to comfort, cheer, inform and strengthen us on our journey. They may delight us, or they may come hidden in the form of a problem which in the solving, blesses us. Finding the strength to deal with our reality positions us to heal. God is our wise and loving Friend, and always supportive of our growth. Like a plant thrusting through the dark earth and stretching upward to the sun, the pull we feel toward the light is real. And there is deep purpose in it.

Eight

Lay Your Foundation

Alice in Wonderland said to the Cheshire Cat who was sitting on a tree branch, "Would you tell me, please, which way I ought to go from here?"

"That depends a good deal on where you want to get to," said the Cat.

"I don't much care where —" said Alice.

. . . . . Lewis Carroll

Indeed. That is exactly where many of us are much of the time, scurrying busily on our way to somewhere else, a nebulous place defined best by being 'not here.' While it can be pleasant or even wise to sometimes just 'go with the flow,' if this is our habit we are allowing someone else's agenda to direct our lives—we are reacting rather than taking action. We can do better. Yes, we must work with the current, but use it to get you where you want to go. We are advancing in our journey, seeing clearly now and dealing honestly with the past and the present. Let's get down to business. We know that we want positive change and our desire is strong. What comes next?

You've probably heard this catchy phrase: "Plan your work, and work your plan." Variations of it are attributed to a number of the world's most accomplished people who keep saying it because, as time has proven, it works. It sounds simple enough, but like so many gems of wisdom, it is easy to say and much harder to do. But it can be done, and in some form is necessary to fulfill any objective. There's no getting around it; building anything significant requires forethought and some kind of a plan. Simple or complex, there are many ways to accomplish this. All begin with a foundation.

A foundation is the base upon which everything that follows is built. Its correctness is crucial. In a building, for instance, if the foundation is faulty, it doesn't matter how stunning the architecture is or how dazzling the materials used, if the foundation is not right the structure may be impressive for a time but it will not endure. It is the same in our lives. Thankfully the architecture of our lives is not made of steel and concrete, we can adjust and make improvements as we go along. In fact, growth requires that we do.

When asked what they want, many people would immediately respond, "I want to be a multi-millionaire!" or "I want to be famous!" Or perhaps, "I want a Lamborghini—red!" There is nothing wrong with wanting and having these. On their own they are neutrals with the potential to be used for any purpose. Yet the glittering goals of worldly success—wealth, status, power, fame—are powerful lures to be approached with caution. Everything has a price, so it is important in the pursuit of any goal to be aware of what might be required. If along the way we develop addictions or habits that damage health or lives, there will be regrets. If we lose integrity, if the price demanded is our character, we sacrifice something far more precious than anything we can gain. Fortunately, we human beings have the capacity to learn and change.

In 2004 a handsome, charismatic young man in New York City was living the glittering high life. For ten years his job as a promoter for a high profile night club took him around the world to exciting places with the trendsetters. Money, women, exotic vacation spots, all the expensive toys he wanted—he had it all. Boarding a plane to Africa one day he discovered he felt utterly, absolutely empty. The truth, when he faced it, was that he was an unhappy man. His realized his life was built on a foundation of immediate pleasure and nothing more. Thus began what he calls, 'The redemption of Scott Harrison.'

Scott did a complete turnabout, and his story is told in his autobiographical book, *Thirst: A Story of Redemption, Compassion, and a Mission to Bring Clean Water to the World*, and online at: charitywater.org. He is a brilliant organizer, and now uses his abilities and contacts to construct wells and bring clean water to those in remote parts of the world who suffer greatly from the lack of it. He radiates happiness.

Assuming that our desire is to build wisely and in the interest of contributing to the greater good as well as our own, I suggest that a solid foundation for life planning requires four basic qualities: authenticity, integrity, commitment, and faith. With these in place we can proceed with confidence. Without them, we are likely to build awry. Faith is the cornerstone that holds it all together.

The importance of a good foundation is graphically described in the Holy Bible, Luke 6:47-49, when Jesus tells this story:

47 "Whosoever cometh to me, and heareth my sayings, and doeth them, I will shew you to whom he is like:

48 He is like a man which built a house, and digged deep, and laid the foundation on a rock: and when the flood arose, the stream beat vehemently upon that house, and could not shake it: for it was founded upon a rock.

49 But he that heareth, and doeth not, is like a man that without a foundation built a house upon the sand; against which the stream did beat vehemently, and immediately it fell; and the ruin of that house was great."

So how do we go about building a good foundation? We first need to identify and examine our core values, because when congruent with beliefs they determine who we are and how we live. What is it that is most deeply important to us? These are our core values.

According to psychologists Barb Markway and Celia Ampel in *The Self-Confidence Workbook,* "Values are the principles that give our lives meaning and allow us to persevere through adversity." We can clarify what our core values are by examining our own lives, and observing the lives of those around us. To help with this, Meg Selig at the Psychology Today website suggests that we:

- Make a list of several people you most admire, historically or in your present life, and identify why you admire them. Is it because of their courage, their compassion, their persistence, their loyalty, or . . . ?
- Observe yourself and learn. What are the choices you make, and why?
- Identify patterns in your life. Are there things that are non-negotiable? What are they? Why?
- How do you react to what is happening around you? Your reactions hold keys to your values.

There are no right or wrong answers here, it is a matter of determining what is most important to you. Self knowledge gives us power over the present and future.

Everyone desires peace of mind. Peace of mind comes from being authentic and making good choices. To be authentic means our behavior is in harmony with our core values. Self-worth is directly tied to living in a way that is congruent with our values. When our values are positive and our behaviour supports them, we feel in harmony, confident and strong. When it does not, there is always some level of unease—something is out of sync and we sense it. We cannot feel good about ourselves if we are doing things that go against our deepest values; it simply isn't possible. To function at our best, our mind, our heart and our behavior need to be congruent, harmonious.

As we decide to live true to our values and move forward in a positive way in spite of obstacles, step by step we become stronger, happier, and more capable. Pay attention to what you are feeling about the way you are living. If you realize your life is not aligned with your values, as Scott Harrison did, you can make a change.

It has been said that recognizing there is a problem is halfway to solving it. It is decidedly true that until we recognize a problem we can't fix it—when the problem is identified we can go about making whatever corrections are needed. If the way you are living is just not working for you, you may realize that your values need a makeover. Are they taking you where you want to go? Think it all through, be ruthlessly honest with yourself, and be open to inspiration. Your decisions about your life are under your control.

Core Values and Core Beliefs are sometimes confused with each other, and while they are related, they are different. Core beliefs are how we feel about ourselves and the world. Positive core beliefs such as: "I am resourceful," "I am trustworthy," "I am a caring friend," "Help will be available when I need it," "I am a good communicator," "Most people are kind," and others, strengthen our ability, support our accomplishment and increase confidence.

Negative core beliefs may actually be in opposition to our values. They hold us back with 'self talk' such as: "I'm not good enough," "I never finish anything," "men/women can't be trusted," "people are out to get you," "I always mess up," and other destructive thoughts and generalizations. Often unrecognized, these core beliefs frequently drive our behavior. They can be the cause of dissonance in our lives.

When I first met Paige she was wearing a shapeless brown jumpsuit with "County Jail" stamped in big green letters across her back. She was a blue-eyed brunette in her early twenties, with anger simmering beneath the surface. It was her first time in jail. She was angry at her parents. She was angry at a system that had failed to help her. She was angry at herself, because her way of coping was to escape with drugs, which led to her present situation. Paige typifies what can happen when our values and core beliefs are at odds.

Paraphrasing, this is Paige's story: *"My parents were both alcoholics and I took care of my little brother Sam. Child Protective Services took us out of our home when I was seven. Even though they didn't take care of us I missed my mom and dad. But I was glad to be away from Mom's friend "Uncle Jimmy," who would come into my room and sexually abuse me when Mom and Dad were gone or passed out. I was afraid of him, he was a bad man. Mom and Dad didn't listen when I told them he was hurting me. Uncle Jimmy said I was making it up.*

After that Sammy and I lived in a family with four other children for a while. They were good to us and I got to see what a normal family was like. It was mostly nice. But kids at school were mean, and I acted out and got in trouble a lot. Then the family had to move because the father got a job in a different state, and my brother and I each went to different foster homes.

In the next one the big brother who was fifteen would come into my room at night and sexually abuse me and threaten to kill me if I told anyone. Then he would be all nice in front of everyone. I was so scared of him I never told anybody. But I hated him.

Then I got moved to another place with some people who didn't have a clue about anything and didn't really care—I think they just wanted the money the state gave them. I was going into the first year of high school and that was when I started doing drugs. The people I lived with didn't even notice or care. When I graduated out of the foster system I couldn't keep a job, and started selling drugs. And here I am.

The thing is, I know better. I don't want to be a drug addict, but I am. I don't want to steal and lie and get other people hooked on drugs, but I do it. I feel like nobody cares about what I do and I get so angry and do stupid things that get me in trouble. I know I want my life to be different—sometimes I dream how I wish it was—but I don't have any idea how to make that happen."

Paige's core beliefs about herself and how the world operates have been formed by her experiences, and her behavior is
out of alignment with her core values. She has been victimized
since her early years. Both her parents and the system failed
her. She has made some bad decisions and is feeling the consequences of them with time in jail to protect others.

Hers is an extreme example, yet most of us can relate to
parts of her story: haven't we all made mistakes? Haven't we
all felt alone, hurt and angry at times? Haven't we all longed
for something different without knowing how to get there?
We all need second chances, sometimes several of them. I had
only a few minutes one-on-one with Paige—the opportunity
to do so is rare, and I will probably never see her again. But
I learned her story: she wanted something different, and I
could feel her desire and see the strength in her. I was glad for
a brief opportunity to look in her eyes and tell her so, and tell
her of some helpful resources. Paige needs help to understand
her own worth and potential. She needs support, guidance
and counseling. She needs to know someone cares. There are
mentors and resources to assist her if she chooses to use them.
I pray she will.

Most of us will not face such staggering obstacles, and yet,
despite severe disadvantages, people can and do turn their
lives around. Clarifying our values and identifying our core
beliefs will assist us in laying the foundation for the change
we desire.

One undergirding guideline can be defined by a simple, universal truth that is part of the teachings of every successful culture and major religion on earth: The Golden Rule. It states: "Treat others as you want to be treated." Simple enough, yet challenging to always employ. It takes an open mind and heart and strength of character to receive it, believe it, and put it into practice. It reminds us that both we and others deserve respect. It is a good place to begin a foundation.

In identifying our core values and beliefs and recognizing their impact, we can make adjustments if needed so that they are aligned. Their alignment creates power, and both core values and core beliefs become an asset working together for our benefit.

Establishing a base upon good core values does not mean we will never have challenges, failures or hardships—these come to everyone, but a thoughtful, solid foundation will give us the ability to withstand the storms and learn new lessons that can catapult us forward. Once we have confidence in our foundation, planning is the next step.

If we want to build a house we need complex blueprints with a master set for the general contractor, another set specifically for the cement workers, another for the framers and carpenters, yet another for the electricians, plumbers, and so forth—each specific to their unique responsibilities. Building a life requires a different set of skills, and it is much more important.

It is in our best interest to thoughtfully consider what we want in the different areas of our lives: physical, social, mental, emotional, financial, and spiritual. Where would you like to be in six months in each of those areas? In two years? In 5, 10, 20 years? There are many approaches and resources online and in books and seminars to assist you with the details of this. Find what feels like a good fit for you. If you feel a highly detailed plan is the best approach, then go that route. Others will find a looser approach more realistic because it allows for the unexpected and encourages flexibility. Discover your own strengths and build on them. However you choose to approach foundational life planning, there are specific tools that are especially useful.

A dear friend, Karen Pool, author and life coach, suggests asking ourselves these three searching questions: 1) "What am I thinking?" 2) "What am I feeling?" 3) " What do I want?" These questions are harder to answer than they sound—they require serious, unblinking honest introspection—and they are important. Give yourself the time to do it. Start with one piece of paper for each question and a pen or pencil, and write it all down without editing; you'll go back and finalize after you go through the preliminary thinking/writing creative process as you work your way to the answers. If it's messy at first don't worry—creativity usually is in the process of getting to a desired result, and it's a temporary mess. Make lists, or utilize a mind map with connected circles of thoughts to help you define your ideas. Use as much paper as you need!

While computers are great, the tangible act of handling paper and pen and writing words or drawing diagrams makes a deeper impression on our brain. There is something about physically handling the implements and using our muscles to form the words that forces us to clarify and organize our thinking in a way that is not possible otherwise. Writing things down improves our focus. And ideas and thoughts are fleeting; in our ever-busy minds the mundane often overshadows the important. Writing it down can preserve significant insights or concepts that otherwise may well be lost.

The answers to the three simple questions above will provide an excellent platform from which to define the things you want in your life. As you ponder them you'll find that an answer will lead to an insight, and that to another . . . In the process we may discover hidden fears or doubts of our ability. We may discover we are feeling some reluctance because we need to make changes: it will take real work to reach our goals and, well, being lazy is—easier. We may realize that the old, critical soundtrack with its flow of constant negativity is still running and holding us back. We need to know these things about ourselves and address them to be most effective.

Equally, in this exercise we may very well discover strengths and resources hidden within ourselves we had not realized were there. I would wager that you are much stronger and wiser than you realize. Thoughtfully answering these three questions is an organic process that naturally evolves into more specific goals. Continue as far as you can, using the resources that seem best to you.

Once it feels 'done for now,' schedule a regular review of your objectives once or twice a year to check your progress and follow through. Having all the details in place at the outset is not important or even desirable; if your final destination is a little or a lot fuzzy early on, don't worry. Sometimes it is better that way—it allows room for wonderful surprises! Specific goals will come into sharper focus as you move forward.

Let's say, for instance, you want to hike to the top of Mt. Majesty. From a distance you can see the shape of the magnificent mountain against the horizon. As you draw nearer more and more details come into focus—you begin to see individual slopes and ridges, and as you come closer, trees and boulders. "Aha," you exclaim, "There—I can see the trail!" Just so it will be as you move toward goals in your life.

Remember that course adjustments enroute are part of every journey; even the autopilot on the jets criss-crossing high above the earth arrive at their destination by continuous small corrections. It's built into the plan. So don't worry if your path is not yet clearly defined. You will refine your short and long-term goals as appropriate. You know your direction; take the first steps forward and the path will appear before you. Magical as it seems, it truly will. Begin!

Poet Bobby Burns said: "The best laid schemes 'o mice an' men / Gang aft agley." (The best laid plans of mice and men, often go awry.) Yes, they do. When they do, remember this quote from Victor Frankl: "Between stimulus and response there is a space. In that space is our power to choose our response. In our response lies our growth and our freedom." Or their opposites. In that space between stimulus and response is where decisions are made, and those decisions determine the course of our life.

Everyone's situation is unique, and it is important to be aware of your own. As J.R.R. Tolkien said in *The Hobbit*, "It does not do to leave a live dragon out of your calculations if you live near him." We must consider the dragons in whatever form they may loom. Even so, it isn't possible to plan for every scenario, and often when challenges come they are something we never anticipated. Be aware, be wise, and trust that you can find the strength and resources to deal with problems when they come. You will.

Probably the hardest part of the whole process is self-discipline, and it is vital to achievement. We'll make little progress without it. Still, remember that expecting perfection of yourself or others is unrealistic, and hinders growth. Just keep trying—you will advance. As you do you will gain confidence in your own judgement and in your abilities. Your sense of self worth will increase along with your growing self-reliance.

There is another important foundational factor. When Susan and I met near the Sleeping Maiden lying atop Mt. Timpanogos, we recognized that a common theme ran through our varied experiences: we both have received great blessings as a result of developing spiritual faith and a personal relationship with God. You may choose to call this force The Universe, your Higher Power, The Tao, Spirit—regardless of the belief system, it makes a tremendous difference in our ability to move our lives forward. While some consider it naive to consider God and spirituality, many know from personal experience that faith in God is a powerful asset. Believing there is a Higher Power with our best interests in mind and experiencing His presence in our life is a source of great comfort—for many, this is the deepest source of strength.

It is easy to become distracted as you make plans and move forward. The acronym for 'focus' is helpful: **F**ollow **O**ne **C**ourse **U**ntil **S**uccessful. Keep your objective in view. In Driver's Education many of us learned this lesson: "When you pass close to another vehicle, don't watch it because you will drift toward it. If you are going through a tight space look to the center, not toward the edges, because your vehicle will follow your eyes. Focus on where you want to go."

It is exactly the same as you set your course in life. Of course we must be aware of hazards and obstacles, but if we give most of our thought and energy to difficulties they will grow and enlarge until they seem insurmountable, taking up space in our lives until we can see little else. We can even blot out the sun by holding our thumbs close to our eyes—the sun is still there, but we can't see it. Staying focused on negatives can prevent us from seeing solutions.

Years ago, I enrolled in a Divorce Recovery class that lasted three months. There were ten or so of us, and under the direction of a competent counselor we shared experiences and learned from and gave support to each other. One woman was still married but in a clearly abusive situation and was considering divorce. Her woes were real and many. It became clear as the class progressed that there were resources available and steps she could take to improve her situation. A couple of months later we ran into each other at a store. Hoping for improvement in her life I asked how she was doing. She began again the catalogue of abuses that we had heard many times during class. " Did you try this?" I asked, "Or this?" No, she hadn't, and the marriage was terrible. I felt sympathy for her, and we parted ways.

Over the next year and a half our paths accidentally crossed three more times. Each time the story was the same. After the second time I said, "You know, if you don't *do* something, it is not going to get better. It is not going to change unless you do." She sighed and said, "I know, I know, but—." I saw her again and the story was exactly the same; her focus was still on the negatives and not solutions. The next time I saw her I could tell from a distance that nothing had improved. I slipped off in another direction. For some reason she was either incapable of or chose not to take any action to help herself. Why I don't know, but I could not bear to hear the sad story again.

Since most of us don't have fairy godmothers who will wave their wand and magically make everything better, clearly we must take action ourselves. As you do, remember that rigidity can cause far more problems than it solves; live with awareness so you are able to make changes and adjust to what will inevitably be a fluid situation. Things will crop up that you never expected, good and bad. Be grateful for happy surprises. Don't let the bad ones throw you—it may mean a temporary detour, or you might need to make a major shift— it's all right. Just keep moving forward, be flexible, forgive yourself for an occasional lapse, get back on track and keep the end in sight.

Keep moving toward the light and listen to your inner guide. Expect the unexpected for it will surely come; not many people's lives go just as they anticipated—in fact, I doubt that anyone's does. That is irrelevant. God wants our success and our happiness, He has great things in store for us, and I know from my own personal experience that He will help us. Our contribution is to do what is within our power to do, and have faith as we move forward. His grace often makes up the difference in amazing ways.

Lay your firm, strong foundation of integrity, authenticity, commitment and faith. Make a plan, and expect that you will encounter challenges, hazards and probable detours along the way. Use them as opportunities to learn. With God's help you will overcome obstacles and your sense of self-worth will increase. You will build momentum and your accomplishments and capacity will enlarge. You are the architect and the builder in this greatest of all adventures, creating your own life.

Nine

Change Your Thinking, Change Your Life

"The greatest discovery of my generation is that a human being can alter his life by altering his attitudes."

. . . . . William James

O ur perceptions and thoughts form our attitudes. Our attitude determines how we respond to the events of our lives, and therefore its course and quality.

A story is told of three workmen at a quarry that was providing stone for a cathedral. When asked, "What are you doing?" the first responded, "Day after day I cut stones out of a mountainside." The second replied, "I am carrying stones to earn money to feed my family." The third said, "I am helping to build a great cathedral to the glory of God!" Each were accurate in their responses, yet they perceived the work differently. We can imagine the impact these different attitudes had on the satisfaction each felt about what they were doing, and on the people around them.

In our lives, if we determine that our attitudes are not beneficial, we can choose to change them. Understanding on a deep level what William James said in his above quote and then implementing it, is key to making the forward progress that all human beings instinctively desire. There are forces working against us, and it behooves us to learn to perceive those things that will deter us and how to best deal with them. It is equally important to recognize our own innate strengths and abilities and all the many resources available to help us. In this chapter we'll discuss effective aids to help us successfully accomplish this vital work.

Remember how the process goes: our thoughts and perceptions—the way we view the world, people and events around us—generate emotions which result in behaviors. Therefore, learning to recognize our thoughts and how to change them if we desire, will change our attitude and the emotions and behaviors that follow. Studies have shown that even for people who consider themselves highly logical, it is almost always emotion that drives their behavior. This clearly suggests that controlling the thoughts that produce emotion is the point of most critical importance. You can learn to do this to your advantage. As William James also said, "Follow your heart, but bring your head along!"

There is an additional approach to this: often we can also change our feelings by altering our behavior. We can change our body language and voice, mimicking positive behavior to generate positive emotions: walking energetically, smiling, and simply looking up really can lift our spirits. Standing tall with your hands on your hips, legs slightly spread, does increase a sense of power. Speaking and moving assertively produces assertiveness. As we persist in different ways of moving our body, usually the emotion follows and can be integrated into new, positive behavior.

When something triggers Brittany she furiously stomps about, yells at people, calls them names and throws things. People walk on eggshells around her. Sometimes after she calms down she is embarrassed and apologizes, but relationships and trust have been damaged. And trust is difficult to rebuild. On the other hand, when Jody's feelings are injured she silently draws inward, soothes herself with a dozen doughnuts and a quart of ice cream, calls in sick and curls into bed for a day or two, replaying the hurt over and over.

Both of these responses to strong feelings can be harmful because they cause damage and solve nothing. Yet they are not unusual. Emotions can be powerful and nearly overwhelming at times for all of us. They are part of being human, and can be wonderful, joyful blessings or distressing liabilities. Uncontrolled, expressing negative emotions can have harmful consequences to us and/or our relationships. It is empowering to know that we can learn how to deal with them in ways that benefit and serve us rather than cause harm.

There are techniques to help us do this. As we have already learned, it begins with recognizing the 'negative soundtrack' in our mind that is so familiar we barely realize it is there. Most people have one. Whatever the negative tape running in the background of your mind is, it can and does shape your attitude. It is up to you to determine what that soundtrack is saying and recognize how it is affecting you. Notice what you are feeling and the underlying thoughts that trigger the emotion. Instead of involuntarily sliding into the negative default, when you notice it happening say "Stop," and immediately replace it with a positive word, words or image you choose. You'll feel the difference. Every time you do this you are programming an outcome you desire. With practice it will become automatic.

Let's say for instance, that we find ourselves feeling resentful again toward a certain co-worker. Our process might go like this: "Kendra makes me so mad! She is such a 'brown noser,' always cozying up to the boss. My ideas are just as good as hers, but she always gets the attention—the boss just ignores what I say." Valid or not, you cannot force a change in your co-worker's behavior. However, you can take control of what is happening for you by stopping the tape, changing direction and responding in a reasoning, rational way. Acknowledge what you are feeling. Then take an analytical look at the situation and decide exactly what result you want.

Give yourself time, think clearly, come up with the options that seem best and implement them.

In certain situations, such as a disagreement or confrontation where you find yourself attacked, upset or at a loss for words, calmly state that you need time to think about what has been said and will get back to the person. And do it. By pausing to think rather than simply reacting to an emotion, you are now in a position to determine what action to take that will best improve things. Be willing to think outside the box and expect that you may need to adjust. Stay aware, kind, and focused on the outcome, believing that you will figure out a solution. In his book *Seven Habits of Highly Effective People,* Stephen R. Covey teaches about achieving win/wins in challenging situations better than anyone before or since has done. His work is a resource I highly recommend.

This same process applies to any situation that generates negative emotions: anger, self-pity, frustration, jealousy, hatred, fear, depression—all these and more. Negative emotions are not automatically "bad." Sometimes they are absolutely warranted. But they are usually unpleasant, and while it is important to acknowledge that yes, painful things do happen and need to be faced, wallowing in negativity over and over is counter-productive. What that response does in fact, is to predispose us toward more of the same by deepening and strengthening the neural pathways of the brain that produce negative thinking and behavior.

When a strong negative emotion arises, sometimes it helps to say it out loud: "I am angry about that!" or "I am feeling really hurt," or "This scares the heck out of me." Then draw some deep breaths and consciously, mentally move into a place where your brain is also engaged. Probably a parent or grandparent at some point said to you, "When you're angry, count to ten." It may take counting to twenty or thirty or more, but it is good advice; it gives you a chance to move out of a purely reactionary response into a more reasoned one so that both mind and emotions are involved.

No one is perfect at overcoming the challenges that appear. We simply do our best and keep learning. Events and situations affect people differently and no one can set the response, method or time frame for someone else. While suggestions can be valuable, problem solving, like healing, will go as it goes and take as long as it takes. However experiences may impact us, the essential thing to remember is this: Yes, you will go through bad places, but Don't Stay There! Trying to ignore real distress doesn't work either—like a beach ball in a pool it will pop up here or there again and again until we face it squarely and honestly and process through it.

Figure out what helps you work through upset in a strengthening way and use whatever methods work—go for a run, a long walk outside or go to the gym; go to a movie; meditate; chop wood; talk to a friend; fill a big bowl full of ice cubes, go outside and throw them hard one by one at a wall (very satisfying, and no damage done!); close your eyes and breathe slowly and deeply; do yoga; meet with your pastor or a professional counselor . . . find a healthy release that works for you. Worry generates negative feelings and accomplishes little, so do what you can, trust in the process and let it unfold. Believe there is a solution and that you will find it. You may decide to temporarily shelve a seemingly unsolvable problem, and by relaxing, your unconscious mind comes up with a solution—suddenly, unexpectedly, you know exactly what to do!

As you learn this process and mindfully put it into practise, you will come to recognize when the emotion is based on negative thoughts or false programming by the way it feels, and you will be able to correct it by consciously shifting into a healthy, productive response rather than spiralling down into problematic behavior. Just as a minute adjustment in aim at a target makes all the difference in where the arrow ends up; mastering this mindful approach shifts your trajectory. Before long this response will happen without conscious thought, and you will have learned a practise that is literally life-changing.

Often we are upset because we have unrealistic expectations. It is useful to ask ourselves, "Are my expectations realistic?" We may be surprised to see that given the circumstances and whatever or whoever else is involved, they are not. Then we adjust as necessary.

Janelle's experience illustrates a way to do this. She says: *"My mother never once said she loved me, and didn't show it physically. I would watch my friends' mothers express affection with touch, words and hugs and I yearned for my mother to do that. I ached for her to tuck me in at night and give me a kiss. She never did.*

Finally now, in my forties, I realize that for some reason or other she simply isn't capable of doing this. She is a reserved, private individual who does not share her feelings, nor does she want to. I no longer expect her to. I can't change her so I simply accept the way she is, and appreciate the good qualities she has. Once I figured this out I stopped feeling so bad about it. She loves me in her own way, the best she can, I think. Would I like to have a closer relationship with her? Of course. But I can live with the way things are, and I find other ways to fill that void."

When we find ourselves distressed—whatever form our unhappiness may take—we really have just Three Choices. We can:

- Change our attitude toward the situation
- Change the situation
- Leave the situation

(Some would say there is a fourth choice, which is to do nothing. However, while that may serve temporarily, at some later point you will find that your options are still as above.) You may find that you begin first with approach number one and work your way through to two or three.

Let's say for example that the problem is that your husband Ken habitually drops his dirty clothes on the floor. Using the above solutions, your thought processes might go like this:

1. Change our attitude: "It drives me crazy that Ken drops his dirty clothes on the floor. How hard is it to put them in the hamper, for crying out loud? Obviously, he doesn't care! On the other hand, he comes home so tired—is this worth fighting over? No, not really . . . he does nice things for me a lot. I can pick up his clothes, it only takes a minute." Sometimes the best option is to say, "This really isn't that big of a deal. I can do this and it's all right." Thinking it through, you'll know whether or not that will work for you.

2. Change the situation: "I am really annoyed about his dirty clothes dropped on the floor. I am going to talk with him about it again, kindly this time instead of yelling, and maybe if he understands that it really bugs me he will try harder. Maybe he honestly doesn't realize he is doing it, and we can work out some kind of a silly signal I give, like pulling my earlobe repeatedly, or saying something goofy to remind him. Maybe that will help. Maybe not. Or, maybe I'll tell him calmly that from now on I will only wash clothes that come from the hamper. Dirty clothes found on the floor will be put somewhere out of the way and he can wash

them. We'll find a solution that will work for both of us."

3. Leave/exit the unacceptable situation: "I've had it, I've tried everything, I'm not dealing with this any more."

Dirty clothes on the floor are probably not a good reason to end a relationship. There are, however, behaviors that are. You are the one who determines your boundaries. When behavior causes serious problems for any member of a relationship, it needs to be addressed and discussed with a solution of mutual benefit in mind. If with time and patience the first two approaches do not work, consider 3 as a final solution.

A word of caution about 3: Remember that all people, including ourselves, make mistakes occasionally and are sometimes insensitive, unkind or unreasonable. And people see things from different perspectives. Forgiving each other is also part of being a healthy, responsible adult. Appreciate that there are consequences to choices. Pay attention to your emotions and your reasoning adult voice, and find the wise place in between that honors both. Take as much time as you need to make big decisions; you don't want to leave in a moment of anger and regret it ever after. In the end, you are the only one who can decide what is best for yourself.

While understanding that relationships are an ongoing, imperfect and ever changing process, a desire to reasonably fulfill the needs and desires of both parties should be the objective for both. Some actions, including both physical and emotional abuse and other serious relationship flaws can be and often should be automatic deal breakers. If you are the only one trying to find a mutually beneficial solution, it may mean that you choose not to be around certain people or certain situations for self-protection.

If you feel in danger or at risk in some way, listen to your gut feelings. You may need to get yourself out quickly without going through the first two steps. Use 911, the police, shelters and other assistance you may need to take care of yourself.

We all understand physical abuse, but as discussed earlier, abuse has a broader definition. While emotional and psychological abuse can be harder to identify, professionals often consider them especially harmful because the damage goes deeper and recovery takes longer. Sexual abuse is a category of its own; it is a violation that can have devastating consequences, especially when it happens in childhood. Abuse, in whatever form it takes, can happen in families, in romantic relationships, in the workplace, even in friendships. Abuse of any kind is never acceptable.

There are additional, more subtle pitfalls to be aware of. Toxic behavior in its many forms is capable of causing serious harm to yourself or others. You may find yourself the victim of someone, or it may be something you yourself have learned to use. Either way it is destructive. Some examples are: habitual lying and dishonesty; bullying; a sense of entitlement with a selfish disregard for the well-being of others;

remaining the victim of an abusive situation when it is clear abuse is happening; manipulation; cruelty; passive aggressive behavior; the list goes on and on. You may be so accustomed to toxic relationships that you cannot see them. Pay attention to what you are feeling. Resentment is often a sign you are being manipulated or that boundaries are being violated. If a relationship consistently causes you to feel used, depressed, resentful, demeaned or despairing, you might want to take another look at it. Or, if the problem is your behavior, take responsibility for that and make changes.

We can, and it is important that we do, learn how to recognize and protect ourselves against such toxicity. The ability to do so will come with the heightened awareness of our own growth process, with education and experience, and with a real desire for a positive outcome. Some grew up learning boundaries and automatically implement them. Some of us did not, and have to learn what appropriate boundaries are and how to enforce them. Boundaries are personal. Depending upon the situation, some may at times need to be flexible, and some are inviolate. Get clear about your boundaries, make them known appropriately when and if necessary, and remember that everyone, others and yourself, deserves to be treated with compassion and respect. Treating yourself with respect could require that you remove yourself from a situation where you cannot grow and thrive.

By learning what healthy behavior is and by paying attention, you can recognize red flags warning you of 'Danger

Ahead!" Then you decide the most effective course of action. As we develop skills our confidence grows—it is exciting to learn that we can have control over self-sabotaging, unproductive impulses and actions, and that we do not need to be at the mercy of our past or of those who would use us or cause us harm. Until we develop awareness and self-actuating skills however, we can be like puppets on a stage, reacting and moving about at the whim of an unseen puppet master pulling the strings. As our awareness increases and we learn to recognize what is happening we can do what is necessary, cut the strings and take control of our lives.

As scientific research continues to learn about human behavior and why we do what we do, understanding the Limbic System is invaluable as we progress in making positive life changes. I share the following simplified information from the Younique Foundation's excellent book *Reclaim Hope* (available at https://youniquefoundation.org), and from other sources: The reptilian brain regulates breathing, heart pumping, digestion and sleeping; its function is automatic and unconscious. Just above it, sitting at the top of the brain stem in the center, is the Limbic System. Some call it the primitive brain. Here our instinctual drives and pleasure centers are located. Here is where fear lives, traumatic memories are stored, and the "fight, flight or freeze" instincts are found. Its purpose is to protect us by propelling us into immediate action. When trauma is experienced, especially early in life, it can rewire this part of the brain so it responds to triggers by reacting with an overpowering fear response, even when that is not necessary.

I experienced the Limbic System doing its job when I went water skiing for the second time. I had water skied once many years before, had managed to get up and ski a bit and had enjoyed it. This particular beautiful, sunny day we took a boat into the middle of a lake. As I positioned myself in the water holding onto the tow rope, skis held in proper position in front of me, suddenly I was terrified. My heart started hammering, I froze, gasped and couldn't speak, much less ski—I had to get out of the water *now*. I managed to scramble into the boat and lay there, muscles tensed and quivering, until my body calmed down. I did not understand what had happened or why. It wasn't until many years later, when I learned about the Limbic System, that puzzling episode made sense.

On a beautiful summer day when I was ten years old I nearly drowned in the middle of a small reservoir and was pulled unconscious from the water. Something about being in the middle of the lake that second day of water skiing — perhaps the way the light glinted off the water, or a sense of being in deep water—something—triggered the panic of that traumatic experience from so many years ago. Even though I didn't understand at the time what was happening, my mind and body responded to a perceived danger.

PTSD and panic attacks that some suffer are the Limbic System in action. It can save us, or it can be triggered in ways that impact our ability to function appropriately.

Here is Niki's experience with a triggered Limbic System: *"When I had just turned thirteen a family friend grabbed and inappropriately touched me in the car when he drove me home after babysitting for his family. It really frightened me. And then it happened again the next time, worse. I was so upset and so scared. I didn't know what to do. He was an influential man in the community and would have denied it if I said anything. My parents would have been very angry with me for embarrassing them, and I would have been utterly humiliated. So I never told anybody. I just avoided him and refused to babysit for them again. But I never really got over it.*

After college I moved to a different city. One day a few years later I was grocery shopping when a man came down the aisle toward me who looked like that neighbor and even walked like him. I knew it wasn't the same man, but my heart started pounding, I started shaking, broke out in a sweat and could barely breathe. I ran to my car, locked myself in and sat there trembling. I couldn't go back into the store to finish shopping, and it was a while before I could calm down enough to drive home."

The Limbic System has a job to do. It doesn't reason, it simply responds. It remembers trauma and does its best to protect us, and it can save us when we are in danger. Sometimes though, that can be a detriment rather than an asset.

When it is triggered and functions in a way that causes problems for us, we can learn to cope with it. In my case, if I had understood the Limbic System and how it works I could have recognized what was happening when I panicked in the lake, and using certain techniques could have worked my way through it, but I did not know.

In Niki's case, she has learned about the Limbic System, its function, and how to deal with it. She knows now that when it is activated in a non-productive way there are techniques that will help her 'ground' herself so she can override the fight or flight response of her body. She can stop, draw some deep breaths and think. To help herself do this she focuses on her immediate surroundings, describing the sensory details—what she sees, hears, smells, touches—truly experiencing the present time and place. This shifts what is happening in her brain. Then she can say to herself something like this: "There's my Limbic System, trying to protect me. But think, Niki. That is not the same man. This is not that situation. That was then, this is now. You are safe here, and there are people nearby to help if you should need it. You are here, now, and you are safe." She can breathe slowly and deeply, saying calming thoughts to herself, grounding herself by focusing on the tangible things around her, until the panic passes.

In other words, she can recognize that what is happening to her is a reaction to an old trauma, and when that is unreasonable and affects her normal functioning she can take control of her thoughts, her feelings, and her bodily response.

The reactions may never disappear completely, but she can learn to recognize them for what they are and control them so that they don't control her.

Our triggered responses aren't always so dramatic, they show up in less obvious ways as well. Chronic stress is a by-product of the world we live in; to some degree or another few escape and we may be so accustomed to living with anxiety that it feels normal. Nevertheless, there is a negative impact on our ability to function well, and to our health. There are many techniques to help us with this.

If you are feeling frazzled or tense, here is a simple mental technique that can rejuvenate and calm you: take an imaginary mini vacation and 'go' to a special, safe place that is yours alone. If you want, choose someone to be there with you. Close your eyes and create a 'favorite place' in your mind. Be utterly still, and consciously relax your muscles. Breathe deeply and slowly. Experience 'Your Place' with your senses. What is it like there? Perhaps you feel soft sand beneath your toes, the warmth of the sun on your skin, and hear and see the lacy, white foam of the turquoise sea purling softly onto the beach. A gentle breeze brings the sweet scent of plumeria . . . Or you are snuggling into a favorite blanket near the cozy warmth of a fragrant, crackling pinewood fire as snow drifts down outside the window and silently covers the trees and earth in soft mounds of white. A favorite person is making hot chocolate in the kitchen . . . You decide, and create your own relaxing, safe place with all your senses and simply "be there" for a few minutes. You will come back refreshed.

A massage therapist friend shares additional techniques to lessen stress when it rears up and demands our attention: use cross body movements such as crossing your arms and alternately tapping your shoulders or arms; knitting or crocheting; walking, biking, dancing; these and other similar movements are calming and literally reorganize the way the neurons in our brain fire, pulling us out of the stressed primitive brain into a place that releases tension.

Another powerful way to shift our thinking into positivity is visualization. It can be used as described above when you created your own special retreat in your mind, and also as a means of accomplishment. Athletes have been using it for years, and when properly done it can dramatically change performance. Science has shown that vivid visualizations can impact the brain nearly as powerfully as actual experience. Visualize what you want to accomplish and see yourself performing it perfectly. Using all your senses, how will your muscles feel, what is your frame of mind? What will you see, smell, hear, touch and even taste? Create this in your mind and experience it as fully as you can, again and again. Like everything else of value it takes time and attention, but when you do this you are literally programming your brain and body for success.

Creating Vision Boards is another effective, visual way to shift our thinking: find pictures and words that meaningfully speak to you of what you desire and what you want to achieve. Put them on poster boards placed where you will often see them. One friend uses a white board with magnets and a dry erase pen so she can change components as she wishes. Spend time every day looking at your vision board and speak affirmations out loud, such as: "Yes, this is who I am." Or, "Yes, this is mine!" Engage your mind and your heart and speak with conviction. Create your own positive affirmations or search for them online.

There are different ways to approach this, and all derive power from your belief in what you are saying. One of the simplest and best affirmations is to use the words "I am," followed by the trait or quality you desire. Use pictures, index cards with words, whatever works best, but keep them visible, speak them with positive energy in the present tense, and do it often until you feel their reality. Keep doing it. These are active expressions of faith in yourself and your future. You are rewiring your brain, laying down new neural pathways and replacing negative programming with positive. You are changing your attitude and your belief in who you are and what is possible. As you do, events and energies will literally begin to shift. Change may come quickly or later, but as you stay focused, positive and believing, it will come.

Perhaps the most tried and true approach to a shift in thinking and attitude is to raise our awareness of the needs of the people around us and help as we can.

When my children were small, before the days of cell phones and long security check lines at airports, I was taking the five of them from Denver to California for a visit with my parents. My husband was working and would not be going. I left the house in order, packed for four young children, a baby and myself; got everybody dressed and our assorted gear and luggage tucked into our big Suburban and headed out to the airport forty minutes away. I was worried about making our flight because we were running a little late.

At the bottom of the freeway off-ramp about two miles away from the airport the car engine sputtered, and quit. Stopped dead and would not start. I had just opened the hood—not that I knew what to do, but I was desperately hoping I might—when a pickup truck stopped behind us. A white-haired gentleman climbed out and asked, "What's the trouble?" He listened to my stressed explanation that the car had quit and we were about to miss a flight, and immediately he swung into action. He piled all of us into the cab of his truck, tossed the luggage into the back and pushed out into the traffic. "What's your husband's name and phone number?" he asked, "I'll call and tell him what happened so he can get the car." As we pulled up to the curb at the airport I said, "I am so grateful for your help; I don't know how to thank you." He looked me in the eye, smiled, and said, "You can't. Just help someone else when they need it." I have never forgotten his kind blue eyes, his help and his words. We hustled and made our flight.

From the simplicity of a friendly smile or a neighborly hello to visiting or phoning a lonely shut-in; working on Houses for Humanity in your community; giving Christmas gifts to kids or a family who otherwise might not receive any; teaching English to and helping acclimate a refugee family; assisting at the community food bank or traveling to Africa to build water wells for villages without them, there is a whole world out there where kindness and help large and small is needed. No matter our circumstances, we can all do something to make a positive difference—a double blessing from which the giver and receiver both benefit. And it feels great to do it: science says that helping others actually activates the release of dopamine, the 'feel good' neurotransmitter in our brain. Everyone wins!

We get so caught up in our own busy lives that we sometimes forget, or we may feel that only the grand gestures count and we have neither enough money or time to give. Often though, it is the small things that matter most—simply caring and letting it show in whatever way we are able lifts another heart, sometimes much more than we can imagine. I will never forget the story from a woman we'll call Emily.

One day while Emily was going about her busy life she felt impressed to make brownies and take a plate to a woman she barely knew in her church congregation. Her first response was, "I don't really know her and I don't have time to make brownies. I need to do this, and this and this—." But the feeling persisted, and Emily shifted her plans to mix up the brownies and deliver them. When she arrived at the woman's home no one answered the doorbell. She was about to turn and leave when the door opened a crack and the woman behind it mumbled gruffly, "Hello?" Emily smiled and said, "I thought you might like a plate of brownies. I just baked them for you." The woman hesitated, reached through the door, took them, and shut the door.

"Well," said Emily to herself as she walked back to her car, "I think I annoyed her more than anything! But, okay . . ." She didn't see the woman at church again, and forgot about it.

A few years later Emily received a letter in the mail. It began, "You probably don't remember me, but you brought me a plate of brownies one day, and it saved my life." The writer introduced herself and went on to say that three years ago she had been severely depressed and felt her life was worthless and that no one cared about her. She had made plans to commit suicide, laid out the medication and was preparing to take it, "When," she said, "you came to the door with a friendly smile and a plate of brownies. I decided that if someone baked brownies for me I must be worth something. I put the pills away and decided I could hang on longer. I moved to a different city shortly after and am doing well. Thank you."

Both giving, and receiving with gratitude are right at the top of the list of ways to shift our attitude into positive mode. Truly believing ourselves blessed—and we all are—feeling and expressing gratitude is a powerful way to feel better. Prayers filled with thanks for the good in our lives humble us, lift us up and enable us to feel God's love. As we send prayers of gratitude to Heavenly Father He blesses us with more. He delights in blessing us, and He also expects us to do what we can to help ourselves and others. This process increases our strength, our capacity and our happiness. We become *more*. This is what He wants for us.

Identifying the particular paradigm through which we see the world is not necessarily easy, but it is tremendously important because it enables us to determine whether our attitude is helping us to progress, or holding us back. If we determine it is not helpful we can change it. The power to do so is within each of us.

Remember that when people change for the better, initially there may be resistance from those around them. Be prepared for that. Change often makes people uncomfortable, especially when they do not initiate it. If other members of a hurtful family system or other relationships resist the new and improving you, it needn't hold you back. You can still make that trailblazing change for yourself. Be strong, be wise, be kind, and be committed. Others may resent it early on but will eventually either adjust, be supportive or drop out of the picture. But you will be at peace, knowing you are doing what you need to do.

Carl Jung famously said, "I am not what happened to me, I am what I choose to become." When we choose to change our thinking about ourselves and our potential, when we decide to see the world with eyes toward possibility rather than defeat, we are on the path of life-changing growth. Be patient with yourself and others. We are not upset with a rosebud because it is not yet a rose; we understand that it is in the process of becoming. So are you. So are we all. When you recognize unhealthy thinking and its impact and choose to take positive action instead, you are literally changing your life. You are becoming the Shining Warrior you are meant to be.

Ten

What Is Holding You Back?

"It requires courage to change. Gather your tools, be honest, be willing and committed to doing the hard work, both internal and external. Have faith. As you move forward you will be amazed at what happens . . ."

..... LHC

You understand the concepts, you have the desire and tools to move forward and you are on your way! Or . . . maybe not quite. Perhaps there is still hesitancy; somehow, something is holding you back. You are not alone in this, and it is important to figure out exactly what it is that is causing you to delay. Pull it out into the light and take a good hard look.

Are you still dealing with faulty thinking that tells you that you cannot have/do not deserve the things you desire? Are you so focused on obstacles that you cannot see past them? Do you feel inadequate and uncertain, afraid to make a mistake?

Maybe someone is telling you your dreams are unrealistic. Are they?

Perhaps you are stopped by a compulsive need for perfection, keeping you frozen in place. Would you rather place blame on your circumstances, background, or other people than take responsibility for your future? Do you really want to change enough to do the work it will require? What will others think? Amy is afraid that if she makes the changes she wants she will lose her fiancé; he doesn't like her to do things on her own. Matt doesn't take action because deep down he fears that he will lose his buddies and his 'live for the moment' lifestyle. Who will he pal around with?

This is a time for self-evaluation.

There could be many reasons to hesitate, and most everyone experiences them to some degree. You need to determine your particular challenge. Unrecognized fear is often a large factor in resistance to change. Progress inevitably is change, and involving the unknown as it does, it can be frightening for ourselves or for the people around us.

Michaela says: *My older brother worked hard to earn his MBA at a good university in Michigan where we live. While he was finishing his degree, he and Darcy, who had known each other in high school, got married. He sent out applications to several companies in different cities around the U.S., and got some good job offers. The one he was especially interested in was in Oregon. The job was just what he was looking for with a company he admired, the pay was great and it had real potential for advancement. He was excited.*

Darcy told him she wasn't moving. She had grown up where they lived, her family and friends were in this community, and she wasn't going anywhere. He couldn't find a good job here that utilized his skills, and he finally took a job selling cars near where they live. He earns an adequate living, but his heart isn't in it. He and Darcy are happy I guess, but I've watched the light go out of his eyes. It makes me sad; he is capable of so much more."

How does one solve such a situation? At first glance it seems that Darcy's selfishness is the problem, and it might be. However, as outside observers we only see what we see, and there may be more to the story than is apparent. Only the people involved can figure it out. In the best scenario each is willing to respect each others needs and desires and communicate to find a compromise that they both can feel good about.

A solution that meets the needs of only one party is a poor solution. Do the people in our lives pay a heavy price to be in relationship with us? It is worth serious thought. Obstacles like this and others are challenging; we get comfortable in our own familiar little groove and don't want to be disturbed even when the change may bring benefits.

If you identify fear of change as something holding you back, consider this: Nothing stays the same. Change is a constant for everything in the universe, and you are already participating. The very earth beneath our feet is changing.

Tectonic plates move in a monumentally slow dance in which mountains rise, valleys sink—in the Himalayas two continental plates are in collision and in a sprint of geologic time Mt. Nanga Parbat rises a half-inch every year, while Mt. Everest continues its snow-covered upward reach at a slightly slower rate of 4mm.

The awe-inspiring giant Redwoods grow taller each season twig by twig, while the soaring pinnacles of desert monoliths eroded by wind and weather imperceptibly diminish. The Colorado River cuts inexorably deeper into the bedrock of the Grand Canyon and carries its grains of sand to the sea. Dust whirled away by the desert wind is deposited in another place and ancient civilizations are gradually buried. All is in motion; despite appearances nothing is truly standing still. Nor are we.

A fascinating trip through online scientific sites tells us that the earth we live on spins at a speed of about 1000 miles an hour at the equator, slowing slightly as you near the poles. The planet is rotating around the sun at a rate of 66,000 miles per hour, and our sun and we with it, are moving through the Milky Way Galaxy at a rate of 480,000 miles per hour. The Galaxy itself is spiraling like a gigantic pinwheel at an even higher rate of speed in an ever-expanding universe which scientists now estimate contains 2,000 Billion galaxies— whirling wheels within wheels within wheels in a dazzling, orchestrated complexity. And we, held tight to the earth by gravity, incredibly don't feel a thing. Yet moving we certainly are, snug in our little cocoon of earthly atmosphere.

Around us we delight in the sudden flashing flight of an iridescent hummingbird. A breeze caresses your cheek and trembles the leaves above you. Flowers grow, unfurl into fragrant glowing bloom, and wither. The sun rises and sets in quiet radiance or flaming glory, and if we take the time, we can watch the stars slowly wheeling through the night sky. Nature has its cycles of growth and rest, fast or slow, increasing or decreasing—all is movement, changing in some direction. We experience it in our own bodies. Everything is shifting, continually in flux.

The non-physical trajectory of our lives is the same, we are either growing or declining. Since we cannot stand still and are going somewhere whether we will or not, it is wise to manage what we can control. Or like little Alice in Wonderland wandering about, we could easily end up somewhere we absolutely do not want to be. While trying to force change rarely yields a good result—a tree will grow only as fast as a tree grows—if our desire is to progress, then mindfully choosing a direction and actively moving toward it offers exciting possibilities.

An often unrecognized obstacle to achieving our dreams is the lack of a support system. We may not even realize we need one—many of us feel we have made our own way in the world thus far and done just fine, thank you. Especially if we grew up in a family without one, we may have no concept of how it feels to function in a supportive environment. We might have been told "you're on your own" either with words spoken or implied, and so do not even know what support feels like.

There is a better, more effective way. Back in the day when horses ruled transportation, a standard was established to measure the energy they produced. One horse produced one unit of horsepower. The synergy of two horses pulling together however, created at least three units of horsepower, sometimes as much as five. So it is with people: working together in harmony toward a common objective can accomplish much more than can ever be done independently.

While some people are lazy and purposely let others do the work, this is self-harming behavior that will eventually backfire. Others insist they are completely self-sufficient and need no help from anyone ever. Self-reliance is unquestionably positive and important. However, even when that is our desire, circumstances can force us to turn to others for help. It is then that we find an important truth: there are people willing to assist us when our need is real. What a wonderful thing to learn when one feels utterly alone and clinging on by our fingertips! Knowing when we need help, seeking and receiving it appropriately and gratefully is a blessing. The other integral part of the equation is being willing to give help to others in ways that we can.

So how does one build a good support system? First, you pay attention to yourself and to those around you. Are the people you spend time with positive and encouraging of your growth? Do they lift you up or drag you down? Choose to be with positive people; minimize or eliminate contact with those stuck in negativity, whose agenda is to criticize and bring everyone down to their unhappy level. If you must interact with them, set boundaries. Being honest and being negative are not the same thing, be aware of the difference and their influence. Remember that we tend to become like the folks we spend the most time with, so choose companions wisely.

Be protective of your goals—don't share them with those who will ridicule or give only negative feedback. Be open to meeting new people and cultivate genuine friendships with those you admire for their attitude, accomplishments and approach to life. Surround yourself with those who help you feel good about yourself and support your desire for positive results and change. Be aware of the impact you can have on the dreams of others, and be that positive, supportive influence for them.

We are meant to do our best to help ourselves, and we are also meant to help each other. When we combine our efforts by working with others toward a common goal, everyone benefits and much more can be accomplished. As the beneficiary of other's kindness we feel gratitude, and gladly join the ranks of helpers. It is yet another wheel that goes round—at times we are on one side of the great wheel giving, at times we are on the other side receiving. Both positions are necessary, together they make the wheel go around, and we can all move forward only as the wheel keeps turning.

The ways in which help comes and is given takes sometimes unexpected forms. Here is Dave's experience: *"I grew up in a family of professionals. Everyone was either an attorney or an investment banker. I didn't know what I wanted to do, but I knew I wasn't interested in either of those. When I was in high school I volunteered at a summer camp for inner city kids, and I loved it! I loved working with kids that had never been around mountains, lakes, plants or animals and seeing their excitement and how much it meant to them. Their world opened up and I loved being part of it.*

When I told my parents I wanted to get a degree in Education and teach disadvantaged kids they were horrified. The whole family was like, "Volunteering, okay, but teaching in a public school for a profession? Why would you want to do that, and what in the world will you live on?" Most of my friends thought I was crazy. My parents were not happy about it, but fortunately they did pay for my college.

Most of my professors understood where I was coming from and helped shore me up, especially two of them, and I found other like-minded people who believed in me and what I wanted to do. I didn't need financial help, but emotional support was crucial because I didn't have any from home; what I got there was a lot of grief. Without that emotional support I probably would have given up. I've been teaching now for eleven years in an inner city school district and my family still doesn't understand.

Yes, it is sometimes really tough. No, I don't make much money. I don't hang out at the Country Club anymore. But it's worth it to me. There is nothing more satisfying than seeing students grasp the idea that despite their disadvantages they can learn, they can set high goals and achieve them. Not everyone catches the vision, but some do—they grab hold and go on to do amazing things. There are people and organizations who want to help if you know how to find them, and I specialize in that. To see what these kids can do is inspiring. I am making a difference in a way that matters. I have never regretted my decision."

Very probably many of the students Dave is helping are dealing with friends or family who tell them they'll never make it out of the ghetto and they are stupid to think they can. Yet some do, and thrive. Dave is part of their essential support system.

Nature gives us a good model of cooperative behavior. Scientists are continually finding more evidence of organisms, plant and animal, working together for their common good. Some of the Coastal Redwoods in Northern California grow as high as a 30 story building, reaching 300 feet into the sky. Being in a Redwood Forest is like entering a towering, hushed green cathedral where massive cinnamon red trunks soar skyward as shafts of sunshine filter down through the mist, illuminating shoulder-high ferns and undergrowth on the mossy forest floor. These are the tallest trees in the world. Yet the Redwoods root system is shallow, usually no more than five or six feet beneath the ground. They compensate by sending roots as much as 100 feet away from the trunk where they intertwine and sometimes fuse with the roots of their neighbors, creating a network so powerful it supports these stately giants, who literally hold each other up.

On the southwest bank of sparkling Fish Lake in the Wasatch Mountains of Utah lives the single largest living organism on earth. Pando is estimated to be around 80,000 years old, and scientists come from around the globe to study it. Pando is an Aspen Grove covering about 106 acres. On an October afternoon when the sun is low in the sky, its quivering backlit leaves glow pure, radiant yellow-gold, punctuated by hundreds of slim white trunks standing like sentinels in the gilded air. Pando is one entity. The grove is connected by a root system that clones itself and starts new trees, communicating and sharing nourishment with all its parts to mutual benefit.

We humans see ourselves as individuals, which we certainly are. We admire self-reliance, rightfully so. Yet if we only see ourselves as individuals we are missing something essential. We are all connected to each other, to the earth itself and all life on it. Caring for the mutual benefit of all matters very much.

At a busy major intersection in California near Sacramento, I witnessed something that happened and was over so quickly I could hardly believe I'd seen it. Each of the four streets feeding into the intersection was four lanes wide plus turn lanes. It was rush hour so traffic was heavy, every street filled to capacity. I was at the front of one lane waiting for a red light to change. Suddenly a car quit right in the middle of the intersection and traffic came to a standstill. No one could go anywhere. For a few seconds nothing moved, then men started getting out of their cars from different directions, first one, then another, then more until there were six or seven converging on the stalled vehicle. Together they quickly pushed it into a nearby parking area, one man bent toward the driver, nodded his head, and they all went back to their own vehicles and traffic resumed again. It was an amazing thing to witness—these men were strangers to each other and to the driver of the stalled car. Without any discussion or upset they perceived a need, acted together and quickly solved the problem!

This spontaneous cooperative problem solving was powerfully illustrated on a beach in Florida one July evening in 2017, when around 6:30 a remarkable event took place. In both directions as far as you could see the beach was lined with tall hotels and people enjoying the tropical sun and surf. The life guards had gone home, leaving the yellow "Caution" flags fluttering on their poles.

Two young boys took a boogie board out too far from shore and got caught in a rip current carrying them out to sea. Their cries attracted the attention of two women who swam out to help. A strong rip current can move as fast as eight feet per second, and both these women found themselves unable to get out of it. Family members swam out to the rescue and were also caught, unable to escape. Soon nine people were trapped in the fierce current and being carried farther and farther away from help. Some people on the beach were aware, but unsure of what to do.

One young couple suddenly had the idea to form a human chain to the drowning swimmers—"a picture of it just popped into my head," said the young man later. They started calling bystanders to hold onto each other's arms, stretching out into the ocean. As each person joined the chain on the beach it lengthened and strengthened, extending into the ocean closer to the desperately struggling swimmers. At one point it was estimated that at least 80 people participated. The chain wasn't quite long enough to reach the group in peril. The young couple who started the chain were experienced in rip currents, so they grabbed boogie boards and with a surfer helping, swam out and one by one brought the exhausted swimmers to the end of the human chain, which quickly passed them along until each was safe on the beach. The need was desperate, an ability to think outside the box to find a solution appeared, and strangers working together quickly created the solution. Nine lives were saved. What a marvelous example of cooperation and caring!

An emotionally healthy adult can give assistance when it is needed and accept it in return. No one, virtually no one, can make it through life alone. Science tells us that the need for human connection is as essential as our need for food and water—it is life giving. To those who would abuse this impulse to help others by taking advantage of the generosity of the human spirit I can only say that you may get away with it for a time, but it will come back to you tenfold. Beware. That is a direction with no good consequences.

Without question evil does exist and terrible things do happen. But forming our worldview from sensational headlines is a distortion of reality—the news agencies make their living by grabbing attention with stories of wrongdoing and disaster. Certainly, such events are part of reality and we need to be aware of what is going on, but a too-rich diet of the news can overwhelm with negativity. It is important to remember that for the most part the earth is filled with well-intentioned people, often enjoying and helping each other out with kindness and concern. Rarely does this receive attention, but it is absolutely real, and significant beyond the headlines.

I am most familiar with the U.S., where when there is a natural disaster hundreds or thousands of people show up to help, sometimes driving for days and bringing needed supplies. No one tells them to go, they do it simply because they see a need and want to help. It also happens worldwide—highly organized efforts like the Red Cross, Worldwide Charities, The Church of Jesus Christ of Latter-day Saints Humanitarian Services, Catholic Charities, Jewish and Muslim organizations and more, work together to accomplish tremendous good on a huge international scale. In the U.S. alone more than 1.5 million charitable organizations, foundations and groups of various sizes and approaches are focused on making a positive difference by helping others. It happens also in neighborhoods, in families, and on an individual level between both acquaintances and strangers. Google search 'stories of people helping other people' and you will find millions of worldwide examples at your fingertips—story after story of folks, including children, assisting others in marvelously creative ways. People do extraordinary things. Good and evil exist together in this world, and we choose by our daily actions which side we support.

So what is it that is holding you back from making the progress you desire in your life? As I asked this question one Sunday at the jail, a perceptive inmate answered, "We go after what we want, not what we need." Ah, yes. Don't we all at times? However, if we are not careful, choosing momentary pleasure despite the possibility of unhappy consequences later can literally derail our lives. Of the twenty-two women sitting in my classroom that day, not one of them planned on jail when they were young girls dreaming about their future. Yet somehow or another, choices were made that brought them there. Paying attention to our direction is *crucial*—it can help us avoid the risks of a dangerous or deadly detour. True, life holds no guarantees and some risk is necessary for progress, but awareness of our direction is all important.

At whatever point we are in our lives, it is exceedingly easy for all of us to be distracted by what seems to be urgent taking precedence over what is really important. It seems to happen almost invisibly while we are busy with other things. Life is complicated and unpredictable and we will get off track sometimes. But paying attention and employing self-discipline to make corrections as necessary can help us achieve the goals we really want.

Perhaps it is simple procrastination that holds us back from moving our lives forward, or a bad habit we don't want to let go of. Maybe we expect instant results and are discouraged when patience and more effort is required. Or we may be so accustomed to things as they are that without realizing it, we are closed to new ideas and approaches. Whatever your roadblock may be, if it is holding you back acknowledge it, deal with it, and consciously choose to move beyond. You have the power to do it.

There is another factor that is seldom discussed, often misunderstood, and is frequently a huge barrier to progress. Yet it is crucial for healing and flourishing. This emotion-laden concept is forgiveness. If you are like me for much of my life, the word itself brought up strong resistance.

While I did not think of myself as a victim, I had experienced abuse since early childhood and in my marriage, and finally realized it was neither normal nor healthy. I understood forgiveness in a theoretical sense, sort of, and thought it was a good idea, I just couldn't see how it applied to my situation. I thought that forgiving meant saying, "Oh, it's all right," and then completely forgetting about it and everything goes back to normal. How could I say and do that, when I knew that what happened was not 'alright'?

Verses in Matthew 18:21-22 of the Holy Bible also confused me, when Peter came to Jesus with a question: "Then came Peter to him, and said, 'Lord, how oft shall my brother sin against me, and I forgive him? Till seven times?' Jesus saith unto him, 'I say not unto thee, until seven times: but until seventy times seven."

What? Why? It just didn't make sense to me.

I gravely misunderstood what forgiveness is.

Forgiveness does not require us to say "It's all right," and somehow ignore wrongs that were committed. The perpetrator may never acknowledge wrongdoing, much less apologize. Even so, whether they do or not is irrelevant to us. Yes, certainly it is important for them, but not to us. This is why: Forgiveness is not about a wrong someone did to you; the purpose of forgiveness is to enable your own healing. When we continue to hold onto the pain, anger and injury of the wrongs done to us and do not forgive, it cankers our soul and stops our progress. By holding on to it we allow the situation or the perpetrator to continue hurting us—refusing to forgive is like drinking poison and expecting the other person to sicken and die. The harm is done to us.

Forgiveness does not necessarily mean saying "It's all right," because sometimes it is absolutely not all right. We can forgive and still protect ourselves, legally if necessary, or by choosing to disassociate with someone. We can forgive and still remember what happened and learn the lessons the experience contained. Forgiveness can happen quickly, or require time. The direction is more important than the speed, and when the emotion has gone out of the memory, we know we are healing.

Sometimes people do ask for forgiveness, and it is good and appropriate to say, "I forgive you," and mean it. When there is an acknowledgement of wrongdoing, true remorse and restitution, forgiveness fills both parties with an indescribable sweetness. However, whether the perpetrator apologizes or even acknowledges the wrong he or she has done is irrelevant to your own healing process. You can choose to forgive because you desire healing, growth and peace for yourself.

On the other hand, perhaps we need to forgive ourselves, or ask for forgiveness from someone else. This is equally important. When this is the case we recognize it, we feel sorrow, we make restitution or apology or do whatever we can to make things right, we abandon the negative behavior, change our heart and our course, and with a clear conscience continue on. In whatever way forgiveness needs to be applied in our lives, for our own sakes it is vital that we come to a point when we say, "I am releasing my anger or shame. I will not allow this person or this situation to continue to hurt and hold me back any longer. I choose to release it, put it behind me and move on."

We can spend a lot of energy trying to figure out someone else's motivation for what they did or did not do, but truly, that is their responsibility, not ours. Ours is to set healthy, appropriate boundaries to protect and take care of ourselves and loved ones—this is a vital part of being both wise and caring. We can feel compassion for those who are causing injury without accepting their hurtful behavior. Usually those who harm others are themselves hurting; we can acknowledge that and still protect ourselves against them.

The world is often unfair, sometimes drastically so, and human beings can do terrible wrongs to one another. Our part is to be kind, firm as needed, protect ourselves and others as necessary, make corrections as necessary and find forgiveness for those who cause harm. Doing so can change them, and it will save us. Mahatma Gandhi made a powerful point when he said, "The weak can never forgive. Forgiveness is the attribute of the strong." It may seem impossible at times to forgive, yet it is possible, and it is necessary if we truly desire healing and personal peace.

The final piece of the puzzle of forgiveness comes from trusting God. He understands our wounds, and He has told us that forgiveness for others and ourselves is essential. The Atonement of Jesus Christ makes this possible, and the grace of God makes it glorious. Our faith in Him and His promises will save us.

So again, what is holding you back? Is your challenge external, or internal? If you feel blocked in your progress, take time to figure out what is in the way, what you need to do to overcome it, and do so. In the New Testament of the Holy Bible Philippians 4:13 says: "I can do all things through Christ who strengthens me." He will, and absolutely, you can.

Eleven

Faith And Fear

"Be strong and courageous. Do not be afraid; do not be discouraged, for the Lord your God will be with you wherever you go."

. . . . . Joshua 1:9 The Holy Bible

An acronym for fear is: **F**alse **E**vidence **A**ppearing **R**eal. It is often an excellent description. Occasionally fear is justified. Frequently however, irrational fear lies at the heart of that which holds us back from making the improvements we desire in our lives.

As the Sleeping Maiden Warrior strode forth she was besieged by the threat of fierce claws and sharp teeth of bears, wolves and mountain lions. While the wild beasts that attack and try to stop us might be external, we can be sure that some just as strong will be internal.

Fear takes many forms and the list of possibilities is long: fear of failure, of rejection or pain; of working hard and falling short; of being made to look foolish; fear of standing out from the crowd and being considered 'different,' or of blending into the crowd and being invisible. Fear of success. Fear of nuclear war, or climate change. Of heights, public speaking, of flying, clowns, aliens, snakes, spiders, and death. We're all afraid of something. While some fears are justified and rational, many are not; they are simply a matter of perception. Either way, we feel them. And here we are, thrown into the harsh, cold world without our cuddly blankies. What are we to do?

When fear is legitimate we leave, we fight, or we make corrections—we do what is necessary to avoid physical, emotional, mental or spiritual danger for self preservation. Irrational fears require a different approach. We know that any fear focused upon grows and gains increasing power, and if we allow it, can cripple us. If we are not aware, we can find ourselves in a prison of our own making. We've heard it before: courage is being afraid, pushing through the fear and doing it anyway. That is what is required.

In *The Life of Pi,* author Yan Martel discusses fear. A boy named Pi finds himself adrift in the midst of the ocean on a lifeboat with a few animals including a Bengal Tiger named Richard Parker. Often the tiger rests, sometimes it doesn't, but it is always there, a few feet away. Telling the story later, Pi muses:

> "I must say a word about fear. It is life's only true oppo-
> nent. Only fear can defeat life. It is a clever, treach-

erous adversary, how well I know. It has no decency, respects no law or convention, it shows no mercy. It goes for your weakest spot, which it finds with unerring ease. It begins in your mind, always. One moment you are feeling calm, self-possessed, happy. Then fear, disguised in the garb of mild mannered doubt, slips into your mind like a spy . . . You become anxious. Reason comes to do battle for you, you are reassured. But to your amazement . . . reason is laid low. You feel yourself weakening, wavering. Your anxiety becomes dread . . . Quickly you make rash decisions. There, you've defeated yourself. Fear, which is but an impression, has triumphed over you."

While fear is certainly justified at times, unless it is an emergency we can learn to examine it when it shows up and determine whether or not it is valid. Our limbic system likes to maintain the status quo because the unknown may hold danger. It is true, change does involve risk. But if we choose to never change, we cannot grow. We must face our fears to defeat them, and we can learn important lessons from observing others.

Fae and Sophia are inmates at the County Security Facility where I teach on Sundays. They told me recently of their fear and how they are dealing with it. This was Fae's third time in jail and Sophia's second. Fae has two children at home that she loves, Sophia has been alone. Among the hundreds of other women in the facility they found each other, talked about their troubles and their dreams, and formed a friendship based on an intense desire for change in their lives. Their fear is legitimate: they are afraid of falling back into old ways when they are released—they've done that before and know it ends badly.

They realize that staying out of jail will require real changes in their habits, their hangouts, their friends, and their thinking. Their release dates are similar and they have vowed to keep in close daily touch to support and help each other stay focused on good choices. Looking ahead, they plan to find programs and additional training that will teach and support them, connect with professionals and caring church leaders, and make new friends who support a positive life. They recognize that they need help to succeed, and they are right. They know it will be challenging, but by using all the tools they can gather, having faith that a new life is possible and taking positive action, it is within their reach. They are determined to do it.

Faith is also a powerful support for them. Both Fae and Sophia have developed a connection with God; they told me they have felt His love for them and they know He wants them to succeed. As they spoke of their plans their voices were filled with confidence, and hope shone in their faces. There are obstacles, and they'll probably need to make deep changes in behavior, attitude and lifestyle, but as they stay focused on what they really want and keep making good choices, 'making it on the outside' is within reach.

As we deal with whatever the fear may be in our lives that would halt our progress, we can take similar steps. There are additional specific things we can do to face and conquer unhealthy fear:

- Identify the fear. What exactly are you afraid of? There is no disgrace in feeling afraid, all human beings experience it. By thinking about it further you may be able to identify its source, which can be helpful; knowing our enemy is halfway to defeating him. Figure yours out.

- Surrender. Accept your fear, acknowledge that it exists. Embrace it, see it as a tool, an opportunity for instruction and growth rather than something that controls you. Accept the reality of your situation: what happened happened, and you cannot change it. In acceptance and surrender to your reality you release tension and gain the ability to think more clearly and take control of what happens next.

- In the moment, you can calm yourself by breathing slowly and deeply from your diaphragm. When we are afraid we breathe shallowly, which takes blood from our brains and prepares our muscles to fight or flee. Breathing deeply for several minutes gets blood back into our brains so we can think more clearly.

- Pace yourself and allow time to ponder, consider and plan. Avoid acting in haste unless of course, it is clear that you must. Often ideas need time to germinate.

- Create a support system: surround yourself with people and systems who support your growth in positive ways. Recognize negative influences and avoid them.

- Persist. Don't be discouraged if progress takes longer than you expected. Growth happens in fast and slow cycles and encompasses occasional setbacks. Be patient, and willing to keep working.

- Turn your fear inside out. ie: Instead of concentrating on your fear of flying, be grateful that you can take the trip and arrive at your destination so quickly. Find and focus on the blessing inside the problem.

- Your attitude matters! Think positive. Expect that you will achieve, you will find the help you need, you will overcome and you will succeed!

Most of us are masters of rationalization; we can find endless excuses for not doing something we dread, or for continuing to do something we know we shouldn't be doing. Sometimes there are valid reasons; often not. When we face something new we may find ourselves toggling back and forth between faith and fear, an understandable reaction—they could be called co-workers, both serving a purpose. Our job is to ascertain whether or not the fear is legitimate and the faith well-placed. When we look beneath our hesitation, frequently we will find unreasonable fear wearing one of its many faces.

Fear likes to hide in the darkness; faith is filled with light and hope. Fear stops us; faith gives us power to move forward.

By bringing our fears out of the shadows and into the light of day, we see and define them more clearly. Sometimes we realize that they are ridiculous and they simply disappear like mist in the sunshine. Or we perceive that they are indeed real and need to be faced. When fear is impacting the quality of your life the assistance of a good therapist can also be valuable.

Even though we may not realize it, faith is the force that keeps us functioning every day—it is faith in the future that gets us out of bed in the morning, trusting that our legs and lungs and heart and hands will work as they should, the lights will turn on, the sun will rise, and water will come from the faucet so we can go about our day. Although we rarely think about it, you might accurately say it is faith that makes the world go round—on this interconnected planet all our lives depend upon nature, upon man-made constructs, and upon other people performing their jobs. We could be paralyzed with fear if we didn't trust life would continue in some functional fashion. Yes, sometimes systems or equipment or people do fail, and surprises can blindside us temporarily. But even then, people are amazingly resourceful. Most often, ways are found to adapt and carry on.

The more one learns about the universe and the earth and its systems, the more one recognizes its incredible interconnected complexity, compatibility, and efficiency. To many, the existence of a supreme, organizing intelligence is obvious. While this is a subject about which you will need to draw your own conclusions, contrary to popular belief and often to the displeasure of some of their peers, a great many scientists express faith and a belief in God. A popular perception promotes the idea that science and belief in God are necessarily in opposition to each other, but research shows otherwise. Elaine Howard Ecklund, Professor of Sociology at Rice University states that 77% of scientists outside of universities have a religious affiliation, while 40% of scientists connected with a university do so. A number of scientists attribute their greatest discoveries to inspiration from a divine source.

Astronomer Carl Sagan said, "Science is not only compatible with spirituality; it is a profound source of spirituality. When we recognize our place in an immensity of light years and in the passage of ages, when we grasp the intricacy, beauty and subtlety of life, then that soaring feeling, that sense of elation and humility combined, is surely spiritual."

Wernher Von Braun, the charismatic Father of Rocketry and Space Science, with his vision, intellect and leadership skills was a giant in a field of giants. It was his extraordinary ability that led the world to the moon and into space exploration in the 20th Century. At one point 600,000 employees were focused on bringing into reality what Von Braun knew was possible. In his middle years he turned to God, and spoke gladly and freely about his religious beliefs. He chose for a favorite scripture Psalms 19: 1, which reads, "The heavens declare the glory of God, and the sky above proclaims His handiwork." At his funeral attended by leaders from all over the world, his friend Major General John Medaris said, "His imagination strolled easily among the stars, yet the farther out into the unknown and unknowable vastness of Creation his thoughts went, the more he was certain that the universe, and this small garden spot within it, came from no cosmic accident, but from the thought and purpose of an all-knowing God."

Francis Collins, scientist, researcher, and the Director of the National Institutes of Health, eloquently states, "I have found there is a wonderful harmony in the complementary truths of science and faith. The God of the Bible is also the God of the genome. God can be found in the cathedral or in the laboratory. By investigating God's majestic and awesome creation, science can actually be a means of worship."

It takes courage to speak out for God in an atmosphere that would ridicule such beliefs. Yet there are many who affirm their faith.

Academy Award-winning actor Denzel Washington is an unafraid Christian. In a recent interview speaking especially to young people, he said, "Number one, put God first in everything you do. Everything that you think you see in me and everything you think I've accomplished, and everything you think I have . . . everything I have is by the grace of God. Understand that. There may have been times where I was less than faithful to Him, but He had faith in me."

Jane Goodall, a scientist recognized worldwide for her ground-breaking research gained by closely observing chimpanzees in the wild for more than 55 years, put it this way: "I absolutely believe in a greater spiritual power, far greater than I am, from which I have derived strength in moments of sadness or fear. That's what I believe, and it was very, very strong in the forest."

Faith is a force, and implicit in faith is action. Gordon B. Hinckley, former President of The Church of Jesus Christ of Latter Day Saints, acquainted with God, spoke often about Him, as well as the importance of focusing on the positive as we meet the challenges of life. He attributed this quote to his father, "Cynics do not contribute, skeptics do not create, doubters do not achieve.'" Exactly so. Anyone can criticize; for results, what is required is someone who takes positive action.

With faith you enlist the help of the most powerful force in the universe. Having that well to draw from gives strength and wisdom far beyond our own. The activating power of faith is available to everyone. Whether a famous actor or renowned scientist, forklift operator, business guru, high school drop-out or PhD, such social stratifications are irrelevant to God. Whoever we are, whatever our position in society, He looks not at the surface, but at our heart. He is ever attuned to us. His help may come instantly or later, but it will come in the way He knows best meets our needs. When we turn to Him in faith, we will find that He is there.

Jesse, a young woman in her early twenties, shares her experience:

"When I got into high school I started hanging out with kids that were smoking, drinking and doing drugs. Although my family went sometimes, I decided I was way too cool to go to church. I was quite the typical rebellious daughter for about five years. I did it all. I got pregnant before I graduated and quit high school. I wasn't sure who the father was, but I decided to keep my baby. My parents let me live at home for a while if I would clean up my act, but I couldn't. They ended up kicking me out and they took care of my little girl.

Everything went from bad to worse. Pretty soon I was living in my car. I got a job at Taco Bell and lost it because I couldn't stay sober. The next night I had a flat tire. It was raining hard and I cut my hand changing the tire. I went a few miles and my car quit. It made funny noises and died. I thought it was out of gas and I didn't have any money. I was soaked and cold and hungry and I was bleeding and it was raining like crazy and it was too far to walk anywhere.

That did it. I was just done with everything. My whole life was out of control, and I decided I wanted out. I was sitting in my car planning exactly how to commit suicide. Then I had a feeling I should pray. It surprised me. I hadn't prayed in years, but I said a prayer for help and I meant it. A few minutes later a car pulled up behind me and a guy walks up to my window. He said, "You look like you need help."

He messed around with the car engine for a little while and got the car started. He gave me some antibiotic ointment and a bandage for my hand. Somehow I knew he wasn't going to take advantage of me or anything, he was just being kind. I was a mess. He said, "I don't think I should leave you alone. Is it okay if I stay with you for a while?" I really did need someone to talk to. He stayed with me, listening to me talk and cry and yell for a couple of hours. He just listened. He got food for me and put some gas in my car. Finally he said, "I think you're going to be all right now." By then I felt a lot better and had figured some things out and I said, "Yes, I am." And he left.

From that time on, things started getting better. I learned that night that God cares about me. I felt it, and it changed me. I'm still struggling with stuff, but I don't feel alone anymore. I'm making better decisions and working on staying sober. I'm not there yet, but I am a different person now. I am going to be alright."

Jesse shifted from fear to faith, and it made all the difference. We are always choosing one or the other. Even with just hope, the precursor to faith, we can still move forward. And as we do, additional confidence will come. Choosing faith—in ourselves, in others, in God—gives strength and courage. Choosing fear on the other hand, fills us with darkness and bad feelings. It stymies our progress.

Whether we are at the top of the ladder of success or miles away from it, God cares about what is happening in our lives. In our desire for improvement He expects us to use the resources available to us—our intelligence, our strength, our experience, and learning from the experiences of others. Knowledge about virtually anything is readily available online; our challenge is what to give attention to. Knowing that we will sometimes fall short wherever we are in our lives, God will support everything that enables our growth in a positive way. When we make the effort, He will reach down and give us a hand up.

However, it is important to realize that contrary to what we may hope for and even expect, turning to God does not exempt us from hardships—His promise is not a life free from trouble or pain. A favorite quote is from C. S. Lewis in *Mere Christianity*:

"Imagine yourself as a living house. God comes in to rebuild that house. At first, perhaps, you can understand what He is doing. He is getting the drains right and stopping the leaks in the roof and so on; you knew that those jobs needed doing and so you are not surprised. But presently He starts knocking the house about in a way that hurts abominably, and does not seem to make any sense. What on earth is He up to? The explanation is that He is building quite a different house from the one you thought of—. He's throwing out a new wing here, putting on an extra floor there, running up towers, making courtyards. You thought you were being made into a decent little cottage: but He is building a palace . . . "

Knocking down walls and ripping up floors is a messy, uncomfortable process, but the new remodel is absolutely worth the trouble. God's way is not always easy, but when He is working with us we become much more than we imagined. He promises that He will walk beside us, carry us sometimes, and always be with us. In partnering with Him we are instructed, strengthened and refined—this is the path by which we become the magnificent Shining Warrior God wants us to be. The stronger our faith the more He will interact with us—it is a healing, beautiful, upward spiral. God is absolutely real. He loves us, He supports our growth and helps us through the hard places. And we can come to know this, and Him, for ourselves.

I realize that to some this sounds like a nice fairytale. To billions of believers now and throughout the history of the earth however, it is a truth they undeniably know because they have experienced the love and peace of God for themselves. I believe in Christ and His promises to us. Christians all around the world believe in Christ. There is joy in following Him. You may find your source of strength somewhere else however; each person's journey is their own, and you need to do what feels best for you.

A few years ago a religious leader sat next to a vehement atheist on a long flight. In becoming acquainted they discussed their different life philosophies.

At one point the atheist said to the other, "How can you know there is a God? There is no way to prove it. How can you believe in something you can not even explain?"

The man of religion pondered a while, and then asked, "Do you know what salt tastes like?"

The second man said, "Yes, I do."

"Is salt real?"

"Yes, of course it is."

"Well," said the other, "Pretend I have never experienced salt. Can you explain to me what salt tastes like?"

Of course, it is not possible to explain the taste of salt to someone who has never tasted it. It is a good analogy to help understand how believing and feeling God in our lives can be so absolutely real, and yet impossible to explain to someone who has not experienced it. If we want to know what salt tastes like we can try it and find out for ourselves. It is the same in coming to recognize God in our lives. Trusting only in our senses seems the height of arrogance and foolishness; as humanity grows in knowledge we have learned the realities of much that at one time was unknown, from microbes to distant galaxies. Anyone who really wants to learn if God exists can ask sincerely with real intent and come to know for themselves.

You are on this earth for a reason. You are unique. You are here to develop and learn and grow into the best possible you. There are things that need doing that no one else can accomplish as well as you. Because you are a beloved child of God your soul contains a seed of divinity waiting to blossom. God understands the challenges you face. He knows the reasons for them and He is there, wanting to bless you and waiting for you to turn to Him. He will never force Himself upon you. But if you really desire to know God and feel His love and power in your life, you can.

Fear can stop you; faith can save you. And faith requires action. As you act on your faith it will grow, and as it does your detrimental fear will diminish and become of no importance. Whether your faith is in God or some other belief system, this remains: faith and fear are mutually exclusive, they cannot exist together. Hold them both in your hands and choose: light or darkness, progression or stagnation. Your choice will determine your happiness and your success.

Twelve

You Can Do It!

"Whenever you find yourself doubting how far you can go, just remember how far you have come. Remember everything you have faced, all the battles you have won, and all the fears you have overcome."

. . . . . Robert Schuller

Your struggles will be different than Olivia's, and hers different than Owen's—what is hard for me may be no big deal to you, and vice versa. What we can count on is the fact that along with the joys of life, difficulties will come in all their variety, and while it can be extremely hard to realize it in the midst of pain and struggling, each will be specifically, individually tailored like a well-fitted suit of clothing just for us, each presenting a priceless opportunity for our personal growth. It is in the heat of the forge, the fierce refining fire, that our impurities are burned away. And if we desire it to be so, each time we pass through the fire we will come forth more pure and more closely conformed into the image of our Maker, who suffered more than all, and overcame all. In the economy of God nothing is wasted on our journey, including struggle, setbacks, and pain. It's all about growth.

Even with that understanding and with real commitment, there may come times when we've been working hard and making progress and we bump up against some kind of a problem that stops us short. We try this solution and that, and that, and nothing works. We are absolutely stymied. What next?

Relax. There are things at play here beyond your control. Allow some time and space for things to work out. It may become apparent that you need to forge a different route. Or it may be that the timing is not quite right. Perhaps it is time for germination: after seeds are planted they lie hidden silently in the ground, and to an impatient observer it looks as if nothing is happening. But the unseen magic of growth is underway, and at the right moment the seed bursts and a tiny shoot pushes up through the earth into the sunshine. So it may be for you. Give the universe some room to bring all the pieces together in the proper order at the proper time, and you may be amazed at what will happen.

When you have done all you can and hit a wall, unable to see a solution, give it a rest and turn your attention elsewhere for a while. Put the problem temporarily on a shelf so to speak.

The solution may appear suddenly like a ray of sunshine bursting through a hole in the clouds. In fact, it often does.

Scientists at the University of New Mexico, Northwestern University, and the University of California Santa Barbara are studying this phenomenon and have come up with surprising data. Simply stated, they have discovered that trying to force a solution can actually prevent it from appearing. They call this cognitive inhibition. By trying too hard the answer can disappear, much like trying to see a dim star in the sky— when you look at it directly you cannot see it, you must look off to the side. Ideas and solutions to problems can be like that—the answer will appear when we're doing something else: gardening or showering or walking or something not directly related to the concern. Even though we are not aware and cannot control it, our unconscious brain is working away like mad, making connections and figuring it all out, until, "Eureka!" Suddenly the solution is there.

It can be even more mysterious than that. When you've done your best to no effect, you realize that sometimes the Universe is paying attention and comes to your aid.

When I re-entered school to complete my University degree I was in my mid-fifties and dealing with Myalgic Encephalomyelitis, the painful disabling illness that tremendously limited what I was able to do. The final classes required a semester of on-campus attendance five nights a week with a great deal of walking involved. Even one class was physically not possible because almost always I was down sick and out of commission by evening. Requirements had changed since the last time I checked (my progress was slow) and now I had to take the classes to graduate, but, taking them would put me past the deadline for graduation. It was a puzzle with no answer for me.

From early high school I had wanted that degree. My parents had not been able to go to college and weren't sure it was all that important, especially for a girl, but I was determined to make it happen.During high school I worked two summers, and also created a little art school in the basement, teaching after-school and weekend classes to children. I saved what I earned and my parents helped as they could. After high school graduation off I went to an out-of-state university. I loved it.

At the beginning of my Sophomore year I was invited to participate in a University Student Leadership Conference at a resort in Jackson Hole, Wyoming, and it was fabulous. In November my art professor asked me to place a painting into the Senior Show the following spring. He said it was unprecedented for underclassmen to participate, but he liked the work so much he wanted it in the show. I was thrilled. I was loving all my classes and dating interesting men—the year was off to a wonderful start.

Mid-December my father called to say I would have to drop out of school. I wouldn't be coming back after Christmas. My mother was ill and they needed me to come home to take care of the house and five younger children. Of course I did. Eight months later when she was better, the money I had saved was gone and my father said they were not able to help finance college. So I went to work, first locally, then as an airline stewardess. I took two short leaves of absence from flying to attend summer school at the university for a few more credits, then married and embarked on raising a large family.

Through a long bad marriage, a disabling illness, divorce, and the extremely difficult following years, I never gave up on my dream of graduating from college. When circumstances unexpectedly brought me to Utah just as BYU began offering a Bachelor's Degree through Independent Study, I was thrilled at the prospect that maybe I could complete my degree. And I was scared. Oh, how I wanted that degree—but would they accept me? I had been out of school for so long, and I was exhausted and down sick most of the time—could I even do it?

I took my courage in hand and applied, and was accepted into the program. There was a little child support to help with rent and I obtained financial aid from Vocational Rehabilitation. Later I received an Outstanding Student award which also helped with finances. Lying painfully on my sofa because I was too ill to do otherwise, I worked my way through those classes one or two at a time, with A's in most. At one point I had to drop out for a year because I was so ill, but was accepted into the program again. After ten years in the Independent Study program, graduation was finally in sight! But unknown to me the program had changed, and I bumped up against immovable obstacles.

For me to graduate some specific things had to happen in a particular order, and for a variety of reasons they were undoable. I tried every approach, every avenue, every creative thing I could think of, to no avail. There were requirements, I couldn't meet them, and that was that. Absolutely Not Possible. Set in concrete.

I had waited and worked so hard for such a long time—I was so close! I was out of energy and ideas and there was simply nothing left to do. I grieved, and then said to myself, "You've given it your absolute best, and you're not going to graduate. It just isn't going to happen." And I let go of it and stepped away.

A couple of months went by. And then, unexpectedly, things started to shift. Amazed, I watched as the first obstacle crumbled, then the next, and the next—each one solved in the necessary order, until within three months they had all worked out and disappeared. It was like watching the massive stone walls of Jericho come tumbling down.

I was tested for a math disability. Yes, there was a disability, not large, but definitely there. (I had always suspected it!) As a result, instead of the semester of required classes on campus impossible for health reasons, which were useless anyway because they would have put me beyond the allowed time to complete my degree, a super-condensed Statistics class was offered. It would fill the requirement for graduation. *Inside* the deadline. I took it.

It was a small group, and by far the most challenging class I ever experienced. It was on campus, midday, three days a week. My son drove me from home to a drop off point close to the building, and picked me up after. There was an elevator. The two hour class required intense concentration that gobbled energy and I couldn't stay upright for long, so much of the time I lay on the sofa (Talk about blessings—how many college classrooms have sofas?) and learned from an exceptionally fine teacher and his assistant. I listened, tried to wrap my exhausted mind around the complex foreign concepts, and did the work the best I could.

Most of our grade depended upon an extremely difficult final exam that involved solving several complex problems. It was structured in a way that would show beyond doubt: you either understood the material or you didn't, there was no way to fudge. We had a week to work on it, and then at our appointed time each of us would meet with the professor, show him our work and defend it. I started out with one approach and had spent hours on it when about halfway through, my computer crashed. All my work completely disappeared. I couldn't retrieve it. My computer-savvy son worked hard to recover it and could not. It was just gone. I nearly had a heart attack.

With only three days left I began again, this time with a different approach that had surfaced and seemed a better solution to the problems. I methodically worked through all of them and went, heart pounding and hands sweating, to meet with my professor. Everything depended on this class. I was so anxious I thought I might faint.

I passed! Not only passed but earned a B, which surprised the professor as much as it amazed me. The whole experience, including a computer crash that redirected my approach to the final, was one of manifesting blessing after blessing. When it was over I had completed all the requirements on time for graduation. Only with the help of God.

When I walked to accept my Bachelor's Degree at the age of 67, it was pure triumph—I wanted to dance across that stage and shout "Hallelujah!" I did manage to control myself, but just barely . . . *Hallelujah! Hallelujah!!* Truly, God is in the details of our lives, and His methods and ways are awesome.

Your journey, your story—successes and failures bundled together—is uniquely your own. You have experiences and strengths that enable you to make contributions no one else can do as well as you. They matter. When the going gets hard, and it will, hold on to that. We begin with energy and focus and then—we hit the white water or the tough climb and we're sweating it out, hanging on with everything we've got, muscles aching, blisters burning—and the end seems beyond reach. It is easy then to give up hope. Don't. Hang on a little longer if you can. Or take a break. If you are beating yourself up, ease up. Yes, hold yourself accountable, but be realistic and recognize your limits given your situation; be as compassionate to yourself as you are to a friend you love. If you need to, rest. Breathe deeply. Acknowledge yourself to be a human being with both strengths and weaknesses and know that both are necessary parts of the whole.

Allow yourself to feel what you feel, and decide what you want to do about it. Remind yourself of what you have accomplished and how far you have come, and relish it. Feel and express gratitude for help you've received. When you are ready, jump back in. You will feel opposition, it is built into the equation. When it comes, have faith that with God's help, you can overcome. It is in the struggle that you learn how strong you are. The harder the road, the greater the triumph when you arrive. And you will arrive!

From your example others will be strengthened and inspired and may also choose to grow. As you mindfully move toward a better future you become part of an exclusive club I call the Gateway Generation. These are the people in any family or situation who become aware of problems and choose a different path. They step away from negative patterns and harmful behavior and create something better. They take responsibility for their lives and rise from suffering to strength, forging the way to a healthier, happier, more congruent way of thinking, living and being. They don't expect it to be easy but they know it is possible.

These women and men are the chain breakers of generational dysfunction, patterns that bind and shackle as surely as chains do, learned or handed down from generation to generation. They range from a sour, critical outlook or defeatist attitude to bullying, entitlement, manipulation, cheating, demeaning others, passive aggressive behavior, arrogance and intimidation, and various forms of neglect or abuse. You can be the courageous soul who sees a problem, desires a better way, and walks through the gate to triumphant change.

Like a rock thrown into a pond there is a ripple effect, and family, friends and associates are also impacted. Their lives can be better because of healthy choices you make. Others will see positive results in your life and can decide to follow your footsteps. They will add the strength of their knowledge and experiences, shoring up weak places and smoothing out rough patches to make the path even more sturdy and strong. It becomes a road that benefits many, supporting each traveler in becoming the positive, marvelous person God intends.

There is a powerful key, hiding in plain sight but often overlooked, which unlocks the door to fulfilling our dreams. It is embodied in this phrase: Obedience to God. "What?" you say, "I am not a child! I don't have to answer to anybody!" This is true; you don't. And blind obedience can get us into a heap of trouble. Yet obedience to God is the Great Law of Heaven, and using this key will open the door to unimaginable treasures. Why? Because it gives us access to unlimited knowledge. God knows exactly what needs to happen for our success, and there is no one who desires it for us more than He does. He has His own ways of doing things, and while we may not always understand His methods, trusting Him opens the door to divine assistance as nothing else can.

Let's say you are planning a trip to a specific, far away place you really want to go. You've made your preparations: studied the brochures, watched the videos and done your research, saved your money, gathered your gear, and you are ready. There is another component—someone has to tell you how to get there. You are going to need directions from someone who knows the way, and the more reliable, the better! The journey to becoming your best self is the same. You have objectives for your life: you want interesting things to do, you want friends and loved ones, you want satisfaction, comfort and occasional excitement. You want a feeling of accomplishment and to know you are making a meaningful contribution. You want to enjoy your life and feel happy, secure and at peace. You want to reach the specific goals you feel passionate about. You want joy. These are also destinations.

We have a friend who knows exactly how to get there, the truest friend we will ever have, in God. He gives us free will or agency, which allows us to make choices about how we live, and He will not interfere with that. He knows the desires of our hearts, and the truly good things we want, He also wants for us. And when we really listen, He speaks guidance and comfort to us in our minds and our hearts by a quiet voice inside. He wants the absolute best for us and He gives us directions to guide us there. These come in a variety of ways— answers to prayer; sacred writings, commandments; inspired leaders, teachers, friends and experiences, and whispers from His Holy Spirit. All of this empowers us. When we give our best efforts and partner with Him, we discover that His way leads into greater light, understanding, accomplishment and happiness.

Even so, a journey is made up of continuing challenges, and you may occasionally still feel lost at times. But never fear, you are not alone. You will have help.

A few years ago a woman living in a small, busy city in the Southwest set out for an afternoon of errands. As she drove along Main Street she noticed a tall, rangy young fellow with the slightly scruffy look of the homeless standing on a street corner. She promptly forgot about him and went about her business. Three hours later, errands completed, she drove back through downtown. The same man stood on the same corner, and again he caught her eye. A voice spoke clearly into her mind: "His name is Kevin, and you are to talk with him."

"What?! Really?" she asked in surprise.

"Yes," came the calm answer. She had some experience with that voice, recognized its source, and knew that she would regret ignoring it. So she said, "All right," and began looking for a parking space.

The closest was almost a block away, and as she walked toward the man she said, "You are going to have to help me, Lord, I have no idea what to say." But she walked to the man who was now sitting on a bench, hunched over with his head lowered, his elbows on his knees. "May I share your bench?" she asked.

He glanced up and grunted.

She thought, "He's either drunk or on drugs. Okay." She sat, put out her hand and said, "I'm Linda." The woman was me.

He took my hand, shook it, and said, "I'm Kevin."

And I began talking, asking this and that, just chatting—I have no idea what I said—and he responded.

He was from the Midwest and had been offered a job in Los Angeles. He said goodbye to his home and went to California. When he got there the job had disappeared. He tried for a few months and could not find work that would pay enough to live on. Finally, out of money with no place to live and no car, disheartened, he hitchhiked back east. He had come through our little city on the way to L.A. and liked it, and coming back through, thought he would stay and find work here. He had planned to go to the library to use the computer to search for jobs, but learned it was several miles away with no way to get there. What I thought was drugs or alcohol was a man in the depths of discouragement.

"There's a public computer room at the newspaper office," I said, "It's close, and you can stay for as long as you want. Hardly anybody uses it. Here, let me show you." We walked a few steps around the corner and I pointed to the building one block away.

I glanced into the open duffle bag at his feet, saw two cans of food and asked if he needed more.

"No," he shook his head, "I have more in there."

"Do you have any water?" I asked. The corner was hot in the sunshine.

He didn't. There was nowhere nearby to get it.

I said, "Don't go away, I'll be right back." After driving around I finally found a place to buy water and returned with a couple of bottles. I asked him if he knew where the homeless shelter was. He had asked and he did. I wished him good luck and left. I felt unsettled though, like there was something else I was supposed to do, but I didn't know what.

I was feeling flabbergasted by the whole experience. My husband's office was seven blocks away and I decided to go tell him what had happened. I did, and said, "I know there is something else I'm supposed to do, and I don't know what it is."

Randy leaned back in his chair and steepled his fingers, thinking. "Well," he said, "When I talk with people who are struggling, I often find it helps to talk about forgiveness."

"Yes!" I said, "That feels exactly right!" So back I went. Kevin was still there on the bench, looking better than when I had first seen him.

"It's me again," I said, and we talked. I don't know the words that came out of my mouth, but as he spoke of his family there was pain in his voice. I shared with him my struggles with family, what I had learned about what forgiveness really meant, and the power of its healing. His response told me that it struck home.

Then I said, "Kevin, there is something else really important I need to tell you. I knew who you were before I sat down beside you. Do you know why?" And I told him what had happened: that I was driving down the street running errands, saw a stranger, and a voice said to me, "His name is Kevin, and you are supposed to talk to him." So I did.

"The thing that is so important," I said, "Is this: God knows your name. He knows your name and He cares about you and what you need. You are important to Him, Kevin. He loves you."

When I left he was standing tall, with confidence and purpose. He seemed a new man.

I marveled then and marvel still at the events of that afternoon. I was simply a messenger for what God wanted to do for Kevin. But how blessed I was and how grateful I am for the privilege! Powerful lessons were taught to Kevin and to me. I understood more deeply than I had ever known, that God is aware of and profoundly loves all His children, especially when they are hurting and lost. He is as concerned for us as He demonstrated He was for Kevin. We may feel discouraged and alone at times, but we are not alone—we deeply matter to Him, all the time.

In the *New Testament* of the *Holy Bible*, Saul was a man who severely persecuted Christians, initiating and aiding in their destruction. One day while traveling to Damascus he had a vision that forever altered his destiny. His name was changed to Paul, and he became a fully committed Christian, a fiercely stalwart apostle of Jesus Christ.

In a letter he wrote to fellow Christians (Romans 8: 38-39), he said, "I am persuaded that neither death, nor life, nor angels, nor principalities, nor powers, nor things present nor things to come, nor height, nor depth, nor any other creature, shall be able to separate us from the love of God, which is in Jesus Christ, our Lord."

So it was then, and so it is now. God loves us profoundly. He doesn't love our mistakes but he understands, and He will help us overcome whatever is hindering our progress. We can trust Him. Sometimes He allows us to struggle, knowing that it is by this means that we become stronger and more capable. Sometimes in His mercy He will reach out and save us. And when we are willing, God will use us to bless others, and then bless us with joy in the doing of it.

Exactly how He orchestrates all He does is beyond our mortal understanding—much as a new baby just beginning to discover their hands is unlikely to comprehend their father's work in Advanced Astrophysics, we're just not there yet. But God wants us to be. Knowing that the most intelligent, powerful Being in existence is paying attention to us, rooting for our success and helping as much as possible without interfering with our free will, tells me that we are of more value than we ever imagined.

What you are is a spiritual son or daughter of the living God who created and operates the Universe. When the dark clouds of tribulation press close and you cannot see your way, remember who you are and why you are here. You are on a journey that will try and test and strengthen you, and you are meant to emerge victorious. What you do matters, to you and to the world.

In Moses 1:39 of *The Pearl of Great Price*, during a glorious vision given to Moses on the mount, Moses asks God to tell him concerning the earth and the inhabitants thereof. God declares, "For behold, this is my work and my glory—to bring to pass the immortality and eternal life of man." God's deepest desire is that we achieve our potential and return to be with Him in the Kingdom of Heaven. He will give us His grace for the journey, strengthen and bless us along the way, guide, teach and support us. But the desire and impetus for growth and the work itself must come from us.

Here is the wondrous truth: Being human we all make mistakes sometimes, yet God in His wisdom and mercy provided a Savior. Because we must be fully clean to be with God, Jesus Christ, who is wholly without sin, willingly paid the price for our repented sins. By Christ's Resurrection he conquered death and gave immortality to all. By his Atonement he enables us to be cleansed, healed and perfected so we can be with him and our Heavenly Parents in the glory they desire to share with us. There is no other figure in human history who comes close to the strength, purity and power of Jesus Christ, Savior to all mankind. There is no greater love. If you do not know this most beautiful of all truths, read the *New Testament* in the *Holy Bible* or *The Book of Mormon*, sacred scriptures that testify of Him, with an open heart and willingness to learn.

Does this personal journey of healing and growth require much of you? Oh yes. And there is nothing more rewarding. Be willing to understand your particular challenges, face them head on and gather the tools you need to master them. Know that you can heal from pain, now or in your past, and be stronger because of it. Be brave and honest with yourself and others; build your foundation on truth and integrity. Choose to be positive. Help those around you and notice and express gratitude for blessings in your life. Wisely set goals and work toward them. Build on your strengths. Ask for God's assistance in your life. Know that faith is so powerful it casts out fear. Try it.

Our Sleeping Maiden rising up has served us well as a symbol of awakening and moving from suffering to strength. In actuality she still lies peacefully on her mountaintop. She is after all, made of granite. But we are flesh and blood, and there is nothing holding us down except our own perceptions. Ours is a true journey that deals with real problems.

You know what to do. You have a marvelous life to live and unique abilities and strengths to offer the world. Self-fulfillment and victory await you. Awake, Beloved, and Arise; become the powerful Shining Warrior you are meant to be!

You Can Do It!

Appendix 1

Suggested Readings

T hese are some of the books I have found especially enlightening. My measuring stick is the Gospel of Jesus Christ. Its truths are found in holy scriptures including: *The Holy Bible, The Book of Mormon, the Pearl of Great Price and the Doctrine and Covenants.* Wisdom and truth can be found in many places; the following list represents a variety of approaches. I have listed the books in alphabetical order by title, preceded by the author's name.

- Susan Keippel: *ABC's for Families*
- Dr. Henry Cloud and Dr. John Townsend: *Boundaries; Boundaries Updated; Safe People; Changes That Heal; How People Grow*
- Jeffrey R. Holland: *Broken Things to Mend; For Times of Trouble, Spiritual Solace from the Psalms (includes DVD); Created For Greater Things; To My Friends: Messages of Counsel and Comfort,* and excellent additional addresses available online.
- Melody Beattie: *Codependent No More; The Codependent: Help and Guidance for Today's Generation*
- Robert Burney: *Codependence; The Dance of the Wounded Souls*
- Kerry Patterson, Joseph Grenny, Ron McMillan, Al Switzler: *Crucial Conversations, Tools for Talking When Stakes are High*
- Gary Coxe: *Don't Let Others Rent Space In Your Head*

- Richard Carlson: *Don't Sweat the Small Stuff, and It's All Small Stuff*
- Dieter F. Uchtdorf: *Forget Me Not; The Gospel at 30,000 Feet;* and additional inspiring addresses available in print and online.
- Eric Berne, M.D.: *Games People Play; Staying OK*
- Anne Morrow Lindberg: *Gift from the Sea*
- Charles L. Whitfield, M. D.: *Healing The Child Within*
- John Bradshaw: *Healing The Shame That Binds You*
- Max Lucado: *How Happiness Happens; You are Special,* and many more
- Gary and Joy Lundberg: *I Don't Have to Make Everything All Better; Married For Better, Not Worse;* and more
- Neal A. Maxwell: *If Thou Endure It Well; All These Things Shall Give Thee Experience; That Ye May Believe;* and inspiring addresses available online
- Thomas A. Harris: *I'm OK--You're OK; Staying OK (with Amy Harris)*
- Victor Frankl: *Man's Search for Meaning;* and more
- C.S. Lewis: *Mere Christianity; The Screwtape Letters, the Chronicles of Narnia, The Problem of Pain; The Great Divorce*
- Elizabeth Smart: *My Story; Where There's Hope: Healing, Moving Forward, and Never Giving Up*
- Sheri Dew: *No One Can Take Your Place;* and more
- Wayne Dyer: *Pulling Your Own Strings; The Power of Intention;* and 20 more
- The Younique Foundation: *Reclaim Hope, Empowering Your Life Through Five Strategies*
- Christopher Reeve: *Still Me; Nothing Is Impossible*

- Jack Canfield and Mark Victor Hansen: *The Aladdin Factor*
- Rosamund Stone Zander and Benjamin Zander: *The Art of Possibility*
- The Dalai Lama: *The Compassionate Life; The Art of Happiness*
- Robert F. Leslie: *The Bears and I: Raising Three Cubs in the North Woods*
- Bessel van der Kolk, M.D.: *The Body Keeps The Score*
- Norman Doidge, M.D.: *The Brain That Changes Itself*
- Don Miguel Ruiz: *The Four Agreements; The Mastery of Love*
- Brene' Brown, Ph.D., L.M.S.W.: *The Gifts of Imperfection; Daring Greatly; Rising Strong;* and all her print and audio books
- Og Mandino: *The Greatest Salesman in the World*
- Gretchen Rubin: *The Happiness Project*
- Masaru Emoto: *The Hidden Messages in Water*
- Watty Piper: *The Little Engine That Could*
- Antoine de Saint-Exupery: *The Little Prince*
- Stephen R. Covey: *The 7 Habits of Highly Successful People; First Things First: The 7 Habits of Highly Effective Families,* and several more
- Deepak Chopra: *The Seven Spiritual Laws of Success*
- Elizabeth Tova Bailey: *The Sound of a Wild Snail Eating*
- Eckhart Tolle: *The Power of Now*
- Norman Vincent Peale: *The Power of Positive Thinking*
- Marcia Grad: *The Princess Who Believed in Fairy Tales*
- Khalil Gibran: *The Prophet*
- Francis Weller: *The Wild Edge of Sorrow, Rituals of Renewal and the Sacred Work of Grief*

- Teryl L.Givens and Fiona Givens: *When Souls Had Wings; The God Who Weeps; The Christ Who Heals*
- Jonice Webb with Christine Musello: *Running On Empty; Running on Empty No More*
- M. Catherine Thomas: *Spiritual Lightening; Light In The Wilderness*
- Scott Harrison: *Thirst: A Story of Redemption, Compassion, and a Mission To Bring Clean Water To The World*
- Anne McGee-Cooper with Duane Trammell: *Time Management for Unmanageable People*
- Karen W. Pool: *Transformational Thinking, Imagine Your Life, Discover Your Dreams; Designing Your Life Vision*, and more.
- Denis Shekerjian: *Uncommon Genius, How Great Ideas Are Born*
- Roxanne Black: *Unexpected Blessings; Finding Hope and Healing In The Face of Illness*
- Larry and Valere Althouse: *What You Need Is What You've Got*
- Cheryl Strayed: *Wild: From Lost to Found*
- A.A. Milne: *Winnie the Pooh*
- F. Enzio Busche: *Yearning For The Living God*

Appendix 2

I Have The Right:

- I have the right to be myself.
- I have the right to be safe.
- I have the right to feel what I feel and think what I think.
- I have the right to express how I feel and what I think.
- I have the right to be treated with respect.
- I have the right to have my needs be as important as the needs of others.
- I have the right to not be abused by anyone.
- I have the right to say no.
- I have the right to make mistakes and be responsible for them.
- I have the right to change my mind.
- I have the right to choose what is best for me.
- I have the right to grow, learn, and change.
- I have the right to value my own experience.
- I have the right to choose what I believe and how I live.
- I have the right to privacy.
- I have the right to rest, relaxation and play when I need it.
- I have the right to ownership of my belongings.
- I have the right to sometimes be illogical.
- I have the right to choose my behavior and accept the consequences.
- I have the responsibility to accord these same rights to others.

You may come up with additional rights of your own. Write them here:

- _____
- _____
- _____
- _____
- _____

Appendix 3

For Your Thoughts/ Ideas/Notes